The Secrets of Rosslyn

✠

The Secrets of Rosslyn

✠

RODDY MARTINE

BIRLINN

First published in 2006 by
Birlinn Limited
West Newington House
10 Newington Road
Edinburgh
EH9 1QS

www.birlinn.co.uk

ISBN 10: 1 84158 438 X
ISBN 13: 978 1 84158 438 6

British Library Cataloguing-in-Publication Data
A catalogue record for this book is available from the British Library

Designed and typeset by Iolaire Typesetting, Newtonmore
Printed and bound by Creative Print and Design, Wales

For AJ Stewart

And in memory of
Sandy Irvine Robertson
(1942–1999)

Acknowledgements

The author would like to thank the following people for their help and advice: Deborah Barnes, John Beaton, Stuart Beattie, Baron St Clair Bonde, the Rt Hon. Earl of Elgin and Kincardine, the Revd Michael Fass, Kit Hesketh Harvey, Jenny Hess, Duncan McKendrick, Graeme Munro, John Ritchie, the Countess of Rosslyn, Andrew Russell, Niven Sinclair, Garry and Lorna Stoddart, AJ Stewart and Mark Turner. A special thanks to Aline Hill, who so meticulously edited this book, and to Hugh Andrew, Andrew Simmons, Wendy MacGregor and the staff of Birlinn.

Contents

List of Illustrations

Preface

My instincts were deeply ambivalent when I embarked upon writing this book. Now I am not at all sure why. Let me explain.

Over the past forty years I have attended three weddings, three christenings and a funeral in the small, candle-lit Collegiate Church of St Matthew, otherwise known as Rosslyn Chapel. On such occasions I was aware of the beauty of my surroundings. I was moved by the chapel's intimacy. Prior to the funeral service, I was given the task of lighting the candles, so many of them, in fact, that it took me a full twenty minutes to do so. As the soft light glowed and flickered over the intricate traceries on wall and ceiling, it was hard to believe that this was widely considered to be the epicentre of some great, unearthly conundrum.

Yet, 600 years after its creation Rosslyn remains an enigma, a centuries-old puzzle buried under a bandwagon-load of inventive nonsense. So multifaceted, and brilliantly conceived, is this nonsense, that the more the strands are analysed, the more difficult it becomes to discredit them. Such is the human need for mystery, that the documentation relating to Rosslyn, and its brethren holy sites in France and the Holy Land, has, in recent years, swollen to gargantuan proportions. The result is a breath-taking web of intrigue that spans three millennia to embroil the Catholic Church, Crusader knights, Freemasonry, painters, poets and musicians, politicians and kings. It even dares to question the veracity of the Holy Bible as we know it.

Increasingly under scrutiny is the wealthy Catholic interest group Opus Dei. Lurking in the wings are the sinister Prieuré de

Sion and an arcane Merovingian Royal dynasty, both of doubtful provenance but given fictional credibility in Dan Brown's best-selling book *The Da Vinci Code* and the Hollywood film of the same name starring the American actor Tom Hanks and the French actress Audrey Tautou.

The invention that has taken place to support this ultimate of New Age conspiracy theories, which strikes at the very roots of Christianity, has spawned a veritable skein of wild geese to chase. Riddled with inconsistencies and articulating several manically unfounded allegations, *The Da Vinci Code*, inspired from an earlier, non-fiction source, *The Holy Blood and The Holy Grail*, has fired the imagination of millions.

And Rosslyn Chapel itself is not least among the beneficiaries, or victims, depending upon your viewpoint. Over 2005 it attracted in the region of 120,000 visitors, a figure which is expected to rise even higher in the years to come. Already there are 32,000 associated websites, and the chapel's official website (www.rosslynchapel.org.uk) currently gets an average of 30,000 hits per week.

Under such circumstances, I do not think it unreasonable to question how and why such a diminutive place of worship, so obscurely situated in the north of the British Isles, should have come to occupy such a pivotal role in a Europe-wide web of intrigue. In the following chapters, I shall attempt to make sense of it all, to burrow through the mounds of unfounded speculation and self-indulgent fantasy. The facts, as I have discovered, speak for themselves, and they are no less amazing or compelling than the fiction.

Roddy Martine, Edinburgh, May 2006

Family Tree of the St Clairs of Rosslyn

The principal lines of descent

☘

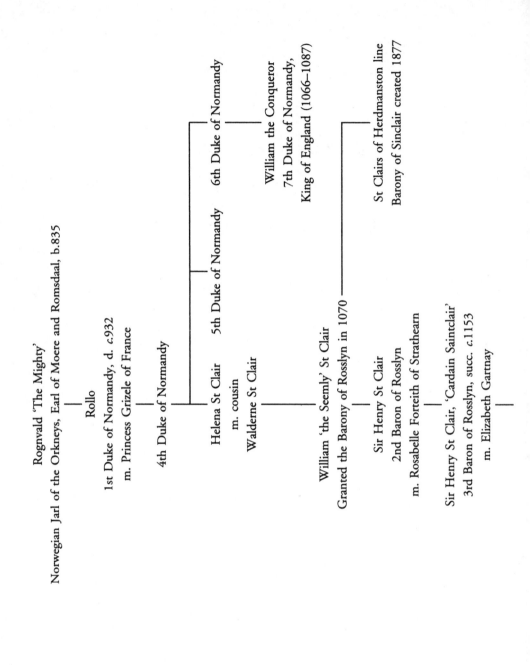

Rognvald 'The Mighty'
Norwegian Jarl of the Orkneys, Earl of Moere and Romsdaal, b.835

Rollo
1st Duke of Normandy, d. c.932
m. Princess Grizele of France

4th Duke of Normandy

Helena St Clair   5th Duke of Normandy   6th Duke of Normandy
m. cousin
Walderne St Clair   William the Conqueror
                                                         7th Duke of Normandy,
                                                         King of England (1066–1087)

William 'the Seemly' St Clair   St Clairs of Herdmanston line
Granted the Barony of Rosslyn in 1070   Barony of Sinclair created 1877

Sir Henry St Clair
2nd Baron of Rosslyn
m. Rosabelle Forteith of Strathearn

Sir Henry St Clair, 'Cardain Saintclair'
3rd Baron of Rosslyn, succ. c.1153
m. Elizabeth Gartnay

Sir William St Clair
4th Baron of Rosslyn, succ. c.1214
m. Katherine Forteith of Strathearn

Sir Henry St Clair
5th Baron of Rosslyn, succ. 1243, d.1270

Sir William St Clair
6th Baron of Rosslyn, succ. 1270, d.1297
m. Jane Haliburton

Sir Henry St Clair
7th Baron of Rosslyn, succ. 1297, d.1331

Sir William St Clair
m. Lady Margaret Ramsay of Dalhousie
d. Teba in Spain in 1331

Sir William St Clair
8th Baron of Rosslyn, succ. 1331, d.1358
m. Isabella Forteith of Strathearn

Sir Henry St Clair
9th Baron of Rosslyn, succ. 1358, d.1400,
& 42nd Jarl and 1st St Clair Prince of Orkney
m. Elizabeth Sparre (dau. and heiress of Malise, Earl of Strathearn and Orkney)

Sir Henry St Clair
10th Baron of Rosslyn & 2nd St Clair Prince of Orkney, succ. 1400, d.1420
m. Egida Douglas (acquired earldom of Nithsdale)

Sir William St Clair
11th Baron of Rosslyn, succ. 1420, d.1484
& 3rd and last St Clair Prince of Orkney

Resigned earldom of Nithsdale in 1455 in return for earldom of Caithness. Resigned Princedom of Orkney in 1470 in return for Ravenscraig Castle
m. (1.) Lady Margaret Douglas   (2.) Lady Marjorie Sutherland of Dunbeath
(dau. of Duke of Touraine)

William St Clair
2nd St Clair Earl of Caithness,
d.1513 at Flodden

Line of St Clair Earls of Caithness

William 'The Waster' St Clair
2nd Lord St Clair of Dysart

Sir Oliver St Clair
12th Baron of Rosslyn,
succ. 1484. d. c.1525
m. (1. Elizabeth Borthwick)
2. Isabella Livingstone

Henry, 3rd Lord St Clair

Sir William St Clair
13th Baron of Rosslyn, d. c.1554
m. Alison Home

William, 4th Lord St Clair

Sir William St Clair
14th Baron of Rosslyn, d. c.1602
Lord Chief Justice of Scotland
m. Elizabeth Kerr

Henry, 5th Lord St Clair

Edward d.1582

Henry, 6th Lord St Clair

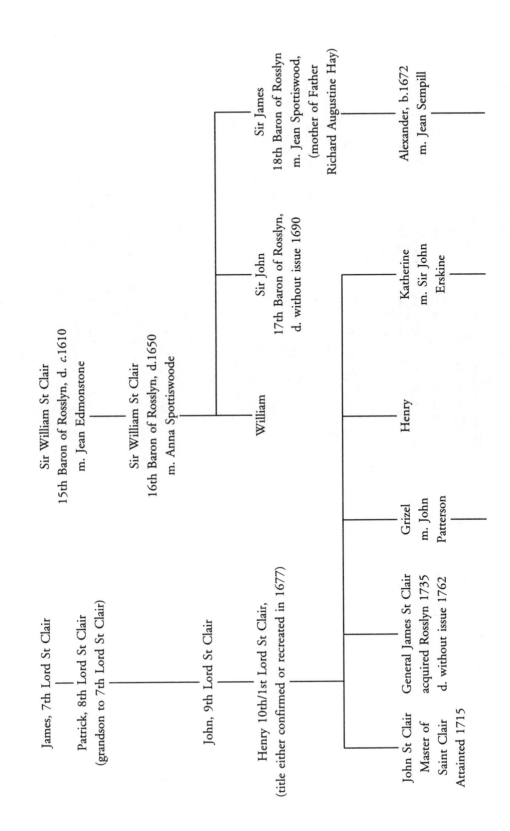

James, 7th Lord St Clair

Patrick, 8th Lord St Clair
(grandson to 7th Lord St Clair)

John, 9th Lord St Clair

Henry 10th/1st Lord St Clair,
(title either confirmed or recreated in 1677)

John St Clair
Master of
Saint Clair
Attainted 1715

General James St Clair
acquired Rosslyn 1735
d. without issue 1762

Grizel
m. John
Patterson

Sir William St Clair
15th Baron of Rosslyn, d. c.1610
m. Jean Edmonstone

Sir William St Clair
16th Baron of Rosslyn, d.1650
m. Anna Spottiswoode

William

Henry

Sir John
17th Baron of Rosslyn,
d. without issue 1690

Katherine
m. Sir John
Erskine

Sir James
18th Baron of Rosslyn
m. Jean Spottiswood,
(mother of Father
Richard Augustine Hay)

Alexander, b.1672
m. Jean Sempill

Colonel James Patterson
Inherited Rosslyn estate
1735 and took name of
St Clair, d.1762

Margaret
m. John Thomson
of Charleton

Grizel Thomson
m. Colonel John Anstruther

Grizel St Clair Anstruther
m. Baron Knut Bonde of Sweden

Line of Lords St Clair

Sir Henry Erskine
inherited Rosslyn estate
from his cousin as son of
General St Clair's sister

m. Janet (Wedderburn)

Sir James St Clair-Erskine,
(nephew of Alexander Wedderburn,
1st Earl of Rosslyn). succ. 1805 as
2nd Earl of Rosslyn, d.1837
m. Henrietta Bouverie

Sir William St Clair
19th Baron of Rosslyn
'The Last Rosslyn'
m. Cordelia Wishart
3 sons & 4 dau.,
all died young
Settled Rosslyn estate
on kinsman General
James St Clair in 1735

Sarah (surviving daughter)
m. Sir Peter Wedderburn,
Lord Chesterhall

Alexander Wedderburn
1st Earl of Rosslyn
(1733–1805)

James Alexander St Clair-Erskine
3rd Earl of Rosslyn, succ. 1837, d.1866
m. Frances Wemyss of Wemyss Castle

|

Francis Robert St Clair-Erskine
4th Earl of Rosslyn, succ. 1866, d.1890
m. Blanche Adeliza Fitzroy

|

James Francis Harry St Clair-Erskine
5th Earl of Rosslyn, succ. 1890, d.1939
m. Violet de Grey Vyner

|

Anthony Hugh Francis St Clair-Erskine,
(grandson to 5th Earl)
6th Earl of Rosslyn, succ. 1939, d.1977
m. Athenais de Mortemart

|

Peter St Clair-Erskine
7th Earl of Rosslyn, b.1958, succ. 1977
m. Helen Watters

|

Lord Loughborough, b.1986

ONE

⟊

Roslin Glen

An earthly paradise

*T*he scenic route to Roslin Country Park is from the A6094 turn-off on the A7 Dalkeith to Galashiels road, where on winter days fine vistas of Rosslyn Castle on the far side of the glen, with its chapel high on the ridge above, can be glimpsed through the trees. The more direct A701 Edinburgh to Penicuik road is rather less inspiring. Yet there are moments. To the north-east is Arthur's Seat, flanked by Salisbury Crags. To the south are the Pentland Hills, fading gently into the distant west. At night, the floodlit artificial ski slope at Hillend resembles a stairway to God. Otherwise, the highway is a narrow, drab affair cluttered with directional road signs.

I wonder what the Scandinavian/Scottish Prince William Sinclair, 11th Lord of Rosslyn, 3rd and last St Clair Jarl of Orkney, Knight of the Cockle and Golden Fleece, and builder of Rosslyn Chapel, would have made of Bilston Glen Business Park with its monochrome warehouses, or for that matter, the affront of Ikea in its monstrous blue and yellow roadside mega-box? Of course, the all-purpose home furnishing store Ikea is Swedish owned. He would have been intrigued by that.

Turning onto the B7006, we find yet another wonder of the modern world, the Roslin Institute (or Roslin Bio Centre as it is signed) where in February 1997 I was sent by the *Scottish Daily Mail* to interview Dolly the Sheep, the first mammal to be successfully cloned from an adult cell. Genetic engineering is another of the miracles associated with this region. Shampooed and fluffed up for the photo opportunities, Dolly was an attractive beast, but, alas, when all of the curiosity died down, her life was short.

Roslin village in the third millennium consists of a fairly typical grouping of early twentieth-century Scottish agricultural and artisan houses. Their predecessors were purpose-built to serve the no longer functioning carpet, bleach and gunpowder industries upon which, from 1834 until the middle of last century, the local economy depended. However, that world has moved on fast. The bleaching works created by Robert Neilson in 1719, which sat on a level below the castle, are long gone. Neilson was a son of William Neilson, Lord Provost of Edinburgh in 1719. He began his career having inherited a great fortune, but then lost it and, as was the custom under such circumstances, travelled abroad. In Holland he was introduced to the art of bleaching linen and, returning to Scotland, soon made a second fortune.[1]

The gunpowder warehouses of Messrs Hay and Hezekiah John Merricks, which fired the British guns during the Napoleonic Wars, are derelict, the coalmines of Midlothian are closed, and where the Henderson & Widnell carpet factory once stood is a large car park. The original factory here was established by Richard Whytock. The velvet tablecloths and tapestries Roslin produced, supervised by David Paterson, a qualified chemist specialising in colours, were in demand worldwide. In 1977, Midlothian County Council acquired the site to create a country park, passing it on during local government reorganisation to Midlothian Council, which maintains it today.

With the run up to the building of Rosslyn Chapel, a settlement was created here as early as 1446. However, this is far from being the whole story of Roslin village. When the work began, the nearest habitation to the castle was to be found half a mile away at Bilston Burn, and so Prince William St Clair built houses to accommodate his indentured employees, imported from as far afield as Holland, France, Spain and Italy. To his stonemasons he paid an annual salary of 40 pounds Scots, the equivalent of £5,400 today; to smiths and carpenters, 10 pounds, approximately £1,240.[2] This might not sound over-generous, but given that housing, fuel, food and clothing were provided free from the estate, it was not a bad living.

In 1456, James II erected Roslin into a Burgh of Barony: a parcel of land granted to a chief tenant in the person of a baron or lord, who held it at the king's pleasure. With its own market cross, a Saturday market, and an annual fair falling on St Simon and St Jude's Day (28 October), Roslin was described as 'the chiefest town in all Lothian except Edinburgh and Haddington'.[3] A Royal Charter was granted by James VI in 1622, and a second later confirmed by Charles I, thus making it legal for commercial activities such as trading and manufacturing to take place within its boundaries. On both occasions, the honour was proclaimed with 'sound of trumpet' at the Market Cross in Edinburgh.

In comparison to all this, the Roslin of the third millennium has become a quiet Midlothian dormitory village of sturdy buildings and practical shops, within easy commuter distance to Edinburgh. Property prices, on the rare occasions that a house actually comes up for sale, tend to be high. 'It's a particularly wonderful place to live during the summer,' says Peter Turner, who has lived here for all of his life. 'The city is only twenty minutes away by car or public transport. There is the garden and, if that is not enough, you can set off for a long walk in the woods.'

Roslin Glen, the hidden valley adjoining the village, is the largest surviving tract of ancient woodland in Midlothian. There is evidence that it was occupied during the Bronze Age, but the names of Roslin and Rosslyn date from a later occupation and originate from the Celtic words *ros*, meaning a rocky promontory, and *lynn* a waterfall or rushing stream; not, as is often claimed, from the Rose-Croix or Rosy Cross of the Knights Templar. Snaking through the gorge is the River North Esk, a dank and frothy ribbon of water rushing north-east from its source in the southern Pentland Hills above the village of Carlops to its confluence with the River South Esk in Dalkeith Park. The secretive nature of this stream adds to the romance of the surrounding terrain as it spills through deep gorges flanked by private estates which, for the most part, remain out of sight to the casual observer. Today, the more accessible Powdermills section and lower glen are managed by Midlothian Ranger Service.

For no apparent reason, other than curiosity, I have been exploring these wooded riverbanks since I was an adolescent. A sucker for Gothic romance, I find myself irresistibly drawn to waterfalls, ravines and mystical woodland, and the experience of stepping into this glen through the rugged archway below the bridge at Rosslyn Castle is the stuff of childhood dreams. The leafy paths that lead up above the water, not to mention the more hazardous, often muddy tracks on the edge of the eastern riverbank, cry out to be explored. No wonder the poet Robert Burns and his friend the painter Alexander Nasmyth came here to muse and daub. No wonder the poet William Wordsworth and his sister Dorothy were spellbound when they visited Sir Walter Scott at his nearby Lasswade cottage in 1803. Roslin's reputation as an outstanding place of Gothic beauty never fails to impress. Generations of artists have been dazzled and inspired by the juxtaposition of castle and river gorge. JMW Turner's exquisite watercolour hangs in the Indianapolis Museum of Art. *The Mermaid's Haunt*, Julius Caesar Ibbetson's more eclectic 1804 vision of the glen, with naiads on the riverbanks and Hawthornden Castle towering above, can be seen at the Victoria and Albert Museum in London.

Centuries ago, a proportion of the valley of the River North Esk between Roslin and the cliffs of Hawthornden may well have formed a broad loch which skirted the site of the present Rosslyn Castle. The low-lying piece of marshy land to the north-west of the castle is known locally as the Stanks and encloses a small hillock known as the Goose's Mound. The name Stanks means stagnant pool, or open drain, suggesting that the water of the loch must have drained away through some natural, and perhaps sudden, collapse of ground. It is linked etymologically to the French word *étang*, meaning pond.

Lochans were plentiful throughout the Lowlands of mediaeval Scotland. From the heights of Edinburgh Castle could be seen no less than seven expanses of inland water, all long since drained. In the case of Roslin Glen, the evidence suggests that a large quantity of water from the hairpin bend beyond today's car park to the Lynn stretch which circles the castle has over the centuries filtered off through natural erosion. But other influences have also made a significant contribution towards the river's configuration. From its source high up in the Pentland Hills near Boarstone and Easter Cairnhill, and the boundary line between Midlothian and Tweeddale, the waters of the River North Esk were gathered into a reservoir in 1859 by the engineer Thomas Stevenson, father of the author Robert Louis Stevenson, who had been contracted to supply water and power to the paper mills on the river's banks.[4] Inevitably, this would have affected the flow downstream, but prior to this, during the late seventeenth century, much of the remaining pool of water in Roslin Glen had been diverted to make way for the powder mill, the later carpet factory and the glen cottages. Whatever the exact details of the past, and however the process of change occurred, what is clearly evident today is just how lush and fertile the glen remains.

To the north-west of the footpath beneath the castle is the slope known as the Orchard; further north is the grassy slope of College Hill with the chapel high above. A stone slab on the walkway marks the spot from which General George Monck and his Cromwellian army pounded the castle walls in the autumn of 1650. From nearby, the pathway climbs to skirt the so-called Lovers' Leap, which juts out high above the river gorge. Low on the rock face here can be seen the crude carving of a face, human or monkey, or, as some insist, a fish. Is this a gypsy homage to the chapel carvings, or the work of a long-ago apprentice mason practising his craft? Nobody appears to know its provenance.

On the far side of the river, cut high into the cliff face, are the caves of the Gorton Estate, the most prominent of which is known as 'Wallace's Cave', implying that the freedom fighter Sir William Wallace took shelter here during Scotland's Wars of Independence. If this is true, then it would most likely have been before the Battle of Roslin in 1303. Perhaps, however, it was later, since there is no firm evidence to confirm that he took part in this particular skirmish.

Later that same century, however, Sir Alexander Ramsay of Dalhousie definitely did make good use of these same caves as a hideout for his freedom fighters. Friend of Robert the Bruce and staunch supporter of Bruce's son, David II of Scotland, Ramsay quartered up to seventy men in these burrows, and led forays as far south as Northumberland.[5] However, anyone planning an excursion here from the Roslin Glen footpath should be forewarned. First you have to cross the river, then climb steeply up the precipitous rock face in which they are to be found.

The Hawthornden Estate above the steep west bank of the North Esk ranks equally with Rosslyn as a place of unique and extraordinary beauty. In early spring the woodland walks are flanked by a carpet of snowdrops and daffodils; when summer comes, the rhododendrons bloom as in their native Himalaya mountains. Looming distant always are the Pentland Hills, pale and undulating on the watery skyline. Nothing much remains of the original fifteenth-century tower house, but in 1638 the celebrated poet William Drummond built himself a fine mansion with gables and a turret on the site. This seventeenth-century building, situated 100 feet above the river, has survived intact.

What has always interested me most, however, is not so much Hawthornden Castle, or its association with the first Scottish poet to write in pure English, but the network of man-made caves which lie immediately below its walls and are said to be of Pictish provenance. These are entered through a locked, low door on the west end of the castle's exterior façade. A second, lower tier is also accessible, but in all probability highly unsafe. Connected by long, low passages, the cells on the upper level have been recently strengthened and are lit by electricity. This catacomb is equipped with a draw-well of great depth, perhaps as much as 60 feet, and it is easy to imagine how fugitives might hold out here for months without being discovered. My personal observation is that for comfort I think they would have had to have stood less that 5 feet in height.

Whether the caves were created in Pictish times or later, the hypothesis that the valley might have been flooded at the time of their creation, long before the castle was built, makes them even more intriguing as access to them would in all likelihood have been by boat. Under such conditions, the caves of Hawthornden and those of Gorton, mentioned earlier, would have been virtually impossible to find. Certainly Sir Alexander Ramsay found them during the Scottish Wars of Independence, and perhaps it was during his occupation of them that three came to be named the King's Gallery, the King's Bedchamber and the King's Dining Room, although there is no record of any Scottish king having ever visited here, let alone having stayed overnight.[6]

Similarly, the claim that Prince Charles Edward Stuart and his Jacobite army passed this way on their march south to Derby is unsubstantiated, although Government soldiers certainly searched for him in the neighbourhood following his defeat at the Battle of Culloden in 1746. The only royal connection that definitely cannot be denied is with Queen Victoria, who visited in 1842 and allegedly dipped her hands into the King's Wash Basin, a hollow cut into the rock in the King's Bedchamber.

In 1070, the year of William 'the Seemly' St Clair's charter for Roslin, the lands of Hawthornden were held by the Abernethy family. Not much is known about them, but according to George F Black's *The Surnames of Scotland*,[7] their ancestors were neither Norman nor Saxon, and therefore native, which perhaps gives credence to the idea that the caves below their castle are of Pictish origin. Etymologically, however, the name Abernethy is purely

Celtic. Hawthornden passed from the Abernethys, who also owned lands at Ormiston and Saltoun in East Lothian, in the late fourteenth century, to their nephew Sir William Douglas of Strabrock, whose descendants continued his support of the Royal House of Stewart. In 1513, Sir William Douglas of Hawthornden was among the knights who fought and died with James IV at the Battle of Flodden. During the English invasion of 1545, Hawthornden Castle was fiercely attacked and burned, as was Rosslyn.

It was the poet and historian William Drummond, whose father purchased the estate in 1598, who brought celebrity to Hawthornden, notably when he was visited there in 1619 by his fellow versifier Ben Jonson, Poet Laureate of England. Jonson, contemporary and friend of William Shakespeare, found Drummond seated in front of his house under the Corvine Tree, a large sycamore which stood at the north-east of the castle lawn, and so called by Drummond because of the crows which annually roosted among its high branches. Drummond himself, it appears, was a true Renaissance man, having invented early examples of perpetual motion, military machines and self-navigating boats. After his death in 1649, the house remained with his family, which, in 1760, joined forces with the bloodline of Hawthornden's original owners when Barbara Drummond of Hawthornden married William Abernethy, Bishop of Edinburgh.[8]

After their deaths, the estate passed to a niece, whose husband took the Drummond surname, and was thereafter owned by their descendants until 1970, when it was sold to Mrs Drue Heinz, the widow of the American Heinz baked beans magnate. Today it operates as a writers' retreat and is administered by a private trust. Among those who have sought sanctuary here are crime writer Ian Rankin, and novelists Michael Arditti and Muriel Spark. The poet Drummond would surely have approved.

TWO

☦

The St Clairs of Rosslyn

A Viking-Norman-Anglo-Scots dynasty

*F*undamental to the enigma that surrounds Rosslyn, its chapel and its castle, is the pedigree of its remarkable owners, the Viking-Norman-Anglo-Scots St Clair family, whose sphere of influence during the three centuries which preceded their acquisition of the Rosslyn Estate, and those that followed, embraced not only Scotland, but France, England, Norway and Sweden. With such a diverse pedigree, it is tempting to wonder how they came to be at Rosslyn in the first place. The answer is to be found in a chain of circumstances precipitated by the politics of continental Europe and, to a large degree, pre-determined by the strategic position of Scotland's eastern seaboard and its many marine trading routes to northern Europe.

In an age of supersonic travel it is hard to imagine that people could be mobile a thousand years earlier, in a world without aeroplanes, trains or cars. Yet European nobility and their retainers covered enormous distances on foot, on horseback, and by boat. In the east of Scotland, the Firth of Forth, with Culross and Burntisland on the Fife Coast, and the well-appointed inlets of coastal East Lothian on its southern shores, provided a string of maritime gateways to Holland and the Low Countries. In contrast to today, when mediaeval travellers arrived in Scotland, it was usual for them to arrive directly from the sea, in preference to taking the more hazardous overland routes through England.

In 1068, when Prince Edgar Atheling, Saxon heir to the throne of England, fled north after the Norman invasion of William the Conqueror two years before, he sailed up the Northumberland and Berwickshire coasts and landed at a Fife anchorage which today is known as St Margaret's Hope. Escorting him and his older sisters, Princess Christina and Princess Margaret, after whom the anchorage is named, was William St Clair, a Norman knight, known as 'the Seemly' for his handsome blue-eyed, blond-haired appearance. William the Seemly was to benefit significantly from his association with the Athelings.

The surname Atheling, which was attached to the grandchildren of Edmund Ironside, means noble youth, derived from *adel* meaning noble, and the suffix *-ing* meaning young. Edgar was aged seventeen, Christina, nineteen, and Margaret, twenty, and through their veins coursed the blood of England's Saxon kings. At this juncture, however, it is important to acknowledge that William the Seemly himself was no ordinary hanger-on. He too came of royal blood. The ubiquitous St Clair family of Normandy, Scotland and England are descended from a family of Norwegian jarls (earls) who, towards the end of the first millennium, held dominion over the majority of the islands situated off Scotland's northern coast. Not content with this, Rognvald the Mighty, Earl of Moere and Romsdaal in Norway, had, in the ninth century, well before the establishment of a unified Pictish/Celtic sovereignty, conquered the region of Caithness on the north-east Scottish mainland.

The acquisition of territory was paramount in the minds of these Norsemen, isolated as they were in their chill Scandinavian fiefdoms. In the early tenth century, Rou or Rollo, younger son of Rognvald the Mighty, set his sights on more distant horizons and rapidly embarked upon a murderous expedition far south into northern France, and the Frankish kingdom of Charles 'the Simple'. Having created havoc, but not much else, Rollo was persuaded to sign a peace treaty in return for the dukedom of Normandy. This treaty was signed at St Clair-sur-Epte, and it is from here that Rollo's family and their descendants took their surname.[1]

Thus, a century later, we find that William the Seemly St Clair is none other than a blood relative of William the Conqueror, natural son of the 6th Duke of Normandy, and the very man from whom he and his royal Saxon companions were escaping. And not just a distant blood relative, if one ignores Duke William's illegitimacy, which, it has to be acknowledged, was rather an important consideration in the religious climate of the age. Duke William was the son of the 6th duke and a tanner's daughter. However, being a bastard was relatively commonplace in the Middle Ages. All that was required was a word from the Pope to declare legitimacy.

William the Seemly's mother, Helena St Clair, was the 6th duke's sister, and, in all likelihood, took a dim view of her brother's libido. Moreover, William the Seemly's father, Walderne (or Wildernus), and his mother, were both grand-children of the 3rd Duke of Normandy, and were bitterly opposed to their bastard kinsman's claim to the Normandy dukedom. Unfortunately for them, the Conqueror was not a man to tolerate defiance. Both Walderne and his brother Hamon were killed in the ensuing conflict, the Battle of Vals-es-Dunes, in 1047.

The St Clairs and their cousin, the Conqueror, were principally related to the Athelings through Emma St Clair, the Atheling children's great-grandmother and daughter of the 3rd Duke of Normandy, who had not only married the Saxon Aethelred II, ruler of England between 1014 to 1016, but his successor, the Danish Canute, who was also King of Denmark and Norway. It makes perfect sense, therefore, that Walderne St Clair's son should have sought refuge with his kinsfolk, who by then were in exile from England in Hungary.

However, families are fickle. Another of Walderne St Clair's sons, Richard, appears to have joined forces with his father's enemy to invade England and was rewarded with land in Essex, Kent, Somerset, Cornwall and Devon. Their sister Agnes is reputed to have been married to Robert de Bruis, ancestor of Scotland's hero king, who also accompanied the Conqueror to England. That is not all. Tradition has it that eight St Clair knights fought for the Conqueror at the Battle of Hastings. Within this incestuous context, William the Seemly's secondment to the exiled Saxon and Royal House of Wessex tends to suggest that the Norman Conquest was, in many respects, only the latest stage in an ongoing family feud.

But how and where exactly did the meeting between William and the exiled Athelings take place? Prince Edgar Atheling, Saxon heir to the English throne, and his two sisters were brought up by their mother's family in Hungary. The accepted version of their origin is that the three grandchildren of Edmund Ironside were brought up at the Hungarian Court, and that their mother Agatha was a daughter of King Stephen. However, through research in continental archives, the author Gabriel Ronay has recently established that Edward, Edmund Ironside's son, and his bride were married in Kiev, at the court of Yaroslav the Great, and that Agatha was a niece of the Holy Roman Emperor Henry III.

Unable to return to England at this stage, a civil war having broken out between supporters of Edmund Ironside and Canute, the family were given sanctuary in the retinue of their cousin King Andrew of Hungary. Subsequently, back in England at the court of Edward the Confessor, their grandfather's half-brother, they met up with the future Scottish king, Malcolm Canmore. It was therefore not, as has sometimes been claimed, divine providence that took them and their followers to Scotland when they fled from England for the second time.[2]

It was in all probability at the Hungarian Court that they first encountered William the Seemly. Ten years later, he accompanied them first to England, then, after a further eleven years had passed, to Scotland. When the 21-year-old Princess Margaret married Malcolm III, King of Scots, in 1069, William the Seemly was rewarded with a knighthood and the lifetime gift of the strategic lands of Rosslyn which, then as now, guard the southern frontal approaches to Edinburgh. He was not alone in his good fortune. From England there had been a general exodus of the Athelings' continental supporters, who had taken up residence at their great-uncle's court: members of influential Norman/French families such as Boswell, Fowlis, Fraser, Lindsay, Preston, Ramsay, Sandilands, Montgomerie, Monteith, Telfer and Maxwell. From Hungary came the Borthwicks, Crichtons, Fotheringhams, and Giffords.

King Malcolm was both welcoming and generous to the incomers, and many of them adopted the Celtic/Pict surnames of the lands upon which they were settled: Abercrombie, Calder, Dundas, Gordon, Mar and Meldrum. Bartolf, a Hungarian nobleman, was given the Barony of Leslie in the Garioch, and similar to the way that the St Clairs had taken their name from St Clair-sur-Epte, Bartolf's descendants became Leslies.[3]

Most of what we know about William the Seemly and the early St Clairs in Scotland we owe to Father Richard Augustine Hay, a Roman Catholic priest who lived in the late seventeenth and early eighteenth century. Father Hay was born in Edinburgh, educated at the Scots College in Paris, and became Canon Regular of Sainte Geneviève's, Paris, later Prior of St Piermont-en-Argonne. Roman Catholicism was outlawed by the Scottish Parliament in 1560, but the faith remained strong regardless and, funded discreetly by such families as the St Clairs, seminaries for training Scottish priests were established in Rome, Madrid, Paris and Tournai, the latter eventually moving to Douai, 20 miles south of Lille. Father Hay's stepfather being Sir James St Clair of Rosslyn, he was made chaplain to the St Clair family and towards the end of his life set himself the task of writing a three-volume study of St Clair records and charters. His project, written in Latin, was completed in 1700, and part republished in 1835 as *Genealogie of the Sainteclaires of Rosslyn*. It has recently been edited, translated and republished by the Grand Lodge of Scotland.

The family's wider dimension, however, is infinitely more

complex. In England, they held land in Norfolk, Suffolk, Kent, Sussex, Somerset, Devon and Cornwall.[4] They continued to own land in Normandy and, as the centuries progressed, were to reclaim some of their Scandinavian territories. France, however, was the key to unravelling the dynasty. Following the Norman Conquest, cultural and political links between the British Isles and France were reinforced as never before. Over the eleventh and twelfth centuries, England and Normandy virtually shared the same aristocracy, not to mention the same rulers. By the thirteenth century there were St Clairs established in every province of France and Alsace. They controlled the castle of St-Clair-sur-Epte and Gison, protecting the gateway to Paris, and, while domestic politics inevitably took precedence, it was impossible for them to ignore the interests and intrigues of the burgeoning Holy Roman Empire. At the same time, family ties on both sides of the English Channel, and as far north as Scotland, irrespective of dynastic power struggles, remained strong.

Over the following two hundred years, despite their domestic ups and downs, every European nation, without exception, became embroiled in the Crusades. Among those who responded instantly to Pope Urban II's call for the Holy Land to be liberated from Islam were the Scottish queen's brother, Edgar Atheling, and his companion, Henry St Clair, son of William the Seemly. By then, of course, William the Seemly was long dead. He had been given the responsibility of defending Scotland's Southern Marches against England, and, as aggression between the two countries escalated under the Conqueror's son William Rufus, he was killed during an English raid. King Malcolm immediately confirmed the barony of Rosslyn, and the additional barony of Pentland, upon Henry, which, even in his absence overseas, gave him legal jurisdiction over the territory and its tenancy, but disaster soon followed disaster.

Within a further three years, the King of Scots was mortally wounded at the Battle of Alnwick. Having been given the news of her husband's death, the heartbroken Queen Margaret expired too.[5] In the ensuing seven years, Scotland was ruled over by King Malcolm's brother, Donald Ban, twice; Malcolm's eldest son Duncan for one year; and his second son Edmund, for three years. Stability of a sort was established in 1097 with a third brother, King Edgar, reigning for ten years, followed by a fourth brother, Alexander I, for a further seventeen. While the majority of all of this was taking place in Scotland, however, Henry St Clair was out of the country, heavily immersed in what was to become known as the First Crusade.

✠

THREE

Holy Reliquary and the Legacy of St Margaret

Lost artefacts of the Dome of the Rock

O n 15 July 1099 a heavily armed group of Norman knights forcibly entered the sacred Dome of the Rock in Jerusalem to interrupt the midday prayers of its Muslim occupants. The unarmed worshippers surrendered, but within twenty-four hours all had been slaughtered. The treasures of the Holy Sepulchre were then ransacked.[1] Although no inventory of the contents exists, it is widely held that the Crusaders laid claim to a priceless collection of hidden artefacts intimately associated with both the Old and New Testaments of the Holy Bible. From this terrible episode emanate not only the ongoing conflict between the two great parallel religions of Islam and Christianity, but the baffling sagas of the Ark of the Covenant, the Spear of Destiny, the True Cross, and the Holy Grail, all of which have been linked in rumour and fiction, at one time or another, with Rosslyn Chapel. So how on earth does the sacking of a mosque 3,000 miles away come to have anything to do with Rosslyn Chapel, let alone Scotland?

The Dome of the Rock, the site of a temple built by King Solomon of Israel, around 9 BC, remains to this day a sacred place of pilgrimage for Muslim and Christian alike. It sits astride Mount Moriah in Jerusalem: the stone summit that features in both the

Holy Bible and the Koran; the plateau upon which Abraham, father of the Hebrew race, was ordered to sacrifice one of his sons, Isaac or Ishmael, depending upon which faith he adhered to. It was also said to have been the outcrop from which Ishmael's descendant, Mohammed the Prophet, ascended to heaven. All of this appears very far removed from the Rosslyn Estate of the St Clair family, until it emerges that Edgar Atheling, brother of Scotland's Queen Margaret, had, in 1098, taken part in the siege of the Byzantine city of Antioch,[2] and that Henry St Clair, the son of his friend William the Seemly, had accompanied him. In all probability they would have witnessed first hand and might even have participated in the attack on the Dome of the Rock, an exercise which reverberated around Christendom like a thunder-clap. So what exactly did the Crusader knights find within the Holy Sepulchre of the Dome of the Rock? Why were the spoils of their sacrilege rumoured to be more priceless than gold?

For a start, King Solomon's Temple was built to house the Ark of the Covenant, the gold-encrusted chest said to have been designed to the specification of God. In the traditions of Judaism, there is no greater treasure, but, amazingly, nobody knows for certain what became of it or its contents, the two stone tablets inscribed with His 'Law' and 'Testament', known as the Ten Commandments and considered the most potent symbols of the Old Testament. A tradition exists that Menelik, a shadowy natural son of Solomon and the Queen of Sheba, and therefore ancestor of the Lions of Judah, rulers of Ethiopia, spirited this greatest of treasures away. But nobody knows for sure, and, as at Rosslyn, the answer to the ongoing hypothesis surrounding its whereabouts in Ethiopia is shrouded in uncertainty. Its traditional home, the church of St Mary of Zion at Aksum, remains fiercely guarded and visitors are turned away.

An alternative notion, of course, is that Joseph of Arimathea, the rich Israelite who, on the evidence of the Bible, was Jesus's uncle and who took possession of the body of his nephew following the Crucifixion, exported the Ark and Holy Grail to

Glastonbury in England.[3] Another claim is that they were shipped to Languedoc in southern France by the Knights Templar, and thereafter to Scotland, where they lie to this day within the vaults of Rosslyn.

Or is the Holy Grail, as is suggested in *The Da Vinci Code*, not a drinking vessel at all, but the bloodline of Jesus himself? And are his descendants by his mistress, Mary Magdalene, still to be found living in Roslin village, where they were eventually sent for their own protection? The sheer audacity of *The Da Vinci Code*'s reasoning is as absurd as it is compelling. However, it has to be acknowledged that, collectively, such questions create one of the Western world's greatest puzzles; the stuff of romance, legend, and outrageous exploitation. In comparison, other holy artefacts pale into insignificance.

Two millennia after the Crucifixion, pieces of the Holy Sponge employed to wash the body of Christ on the Cross, can still be inspected in the Basilica of St John Lateran and the Basilica of Santa Maria Maggiore in Rome, at Santa Maria in Trastevere, at St Mary in Campitelli, and at St Jacques de Compiegne in France. As recently as 1993, the alleged foreskin of Jesus, apparently removed following his ordeal on the Cross, was paraded through the streets of Calcata in Italy.

Taking a lead from the Holy Roman Emperors, the German Chancellor Adolf Hitler genuinely believed that he who held the Spear of Destiny, the holy lance which pierced the side of Jesus on the Cross, had the power to conquer the world, and that losing it meant instant destruction. Following the annexation of Austria, his first initiative was to remove what remains of it from its display case in Vienna's Hofburg Museum, which is situated in a former Habsburg palace. In homage to Richard Wagner's 1882 opera, *Parsifal*, the spear was sent to Nüremburg, a mediaeval merchant city favoured by the Nazis as their spiritual centre.

For the Führer, however, the Spear of Destiny represented another, less obvious, but more spiritually immediate, association. At least two thirds of the generals of the Third Reich were of East

Prussian blood and were therefore descendants of the Order of the Teutonic Knights,[4] a spin-off from the traditional guardians of the Dome of the Rock, the Knights Templar. When the Spear of Destiny fell into the hands of the invading American army, Adolf Hitler committed suicide, although, of course, this is purely coincidental. Or was it?

It is intriguing to view a twentieth-century tyrant in the light of this superstitiousness, but in the mediaeval world, the ownership of a holy reliquary was the enjoyment of Divine Grace. When Princess Margaret Atheling arrived in Scotland in 1068, her most prized possession was a fragment of the True Cross set within an ebony crucifix richly ornamented in pure gold, about an ell long (approximately 45 inches). This was no bauble but a substantial object, considered to be a dowry beyond price.

Christian tradition says that the True Cross is that upon which Jesus Christ was crucified at Golgotha. A further embellishment is that it was hewn from the Tree of Jesse, named after the father of the biblical King David, which sprang from the Tree of Knowledge in the Garden of Eden. In the decades following the Crucifixion, the site of the Holy Sepulchre was covered over by a Temple of Venus, part of the Emperor Hadrian's reconstruction programme. Three centuries later, the Frankish/Roman Emperor Constantine, newly converted to Christianity, had the site uncovered, at which time, it is said, the True Cross was, amazingly, retrieved along with two other crosses. Also unearthed were nails believed to have been those which held Christ on the Cross, and Constantine's mother, Helena, had them taken to Constantinople where they were incorporated into the emperor's helmet and the bridle of his horse.

Once identified – by the enactment of a healing miracle, of course – the Cross of the Saviour was enshrined in a covering of silver and committed to the care of the Bishop of Jerusalem. Whether the story of the finding of the True Cross is based on fact or political expediency, the building of the basilica, the Royal House of the Holy Sepulchre was definitely completed during this century, and, more significantly, fragments of the True Cross are known to have been in general circulation throughout Christian Europe at the time. Around AD 455, the Patriarch of Jerusalem sent a piece to Pope Leo I. Two centuries later, another portion was taken to Rome by the Byzantine Pope Sergius I. Towards the close of the Middle Ages, the Protestant reformer John Calvin remarked that there were so many churches claiming to have a piece of the True Cross that they must have had enough wood to fill a ship.[5]

Given the ravages and uncertainties of time, I think it remarkable that anything at all, true holy relic or impostor, survived the successive waves of pillaging that took place for more than a millennium after the death of Christ. During the seventh century Jerusalem was plundered first by the Persians, then by soldiers of the Roman emperor Heraclius. It was next over-run by Islam, and, although religious tolerance generally prevailed, holy reliquaries were considered idolatrous. In 1009 the remainder of the True Cross was hidden by a group of Christians and survived undiscovered until Jerusalem was taken by the Crusaders ninety years later. What they found then was a small fragment of wood embedded in a substantial golden cross, not dissimilar to the one brought to Scotland by Queen Margaret, a gift from her cousin King Andrew of Hungary, and yet another that was in the possession of the Royal House of Wales.

In 1187, Jerusalem was taken back by the Muslim warrior Saladin. This Ayyubid Sultan of Egypt was unlike anything the Crusaders had hitherto encountered. A brilliant general, he was both an astute and educated man, and when he entered Jerusalem on the twenty-seventh day of the Islamic month of Rajab not a building was looted and not one person harmed. In conquering the Holy City, however, Saladin also took possession of the remainder of the True Cross of Jerusalem. Within a decade it too had disappeared.[6]

Which, of course, only served to enhance the reputation of the reliquary brought to Scotland a century earlier by Queen

Margaret. In the Scots tongue, this priceless artefact became known as the Holy Rude, and, following her death, was revered with deep devotion. Jealously guarded as one of the Crown Jewels of Scotland, the great abbey church of Holyrood in Edinburgh was especially built to house it. Over the following centuries, it would be carried off to England twice. On both occasions, members of the devoutly Catholic St Clair family of Rosslyn would play a part in its return, safekeeping, and its subsequent disappearance.

FOUR

✠

The Poor Knights of the Temple of Solomon

Myths of an unlikely relationship

T he Order of the Poor Knights of the Temple of Solomon was founded in the Holy Land in 1118 by Hugh de Payen (or de Payens), a nobleman from Champagne in north-east France. In the alleged association between the St Clairs and the Knights Templar, as the Poor Knights came to be called, much is made of de Payen's marriage to a Catherine St Clair, thought to have been either the daughter or sister of Sir Henry with whom he had served during the First Crusade. Yet in his 1700 St Clair family history Father Hay makes no reference to this, which seems odd if de Payens had indeed married into the family; Hay had already written a brief, not unsympathetic, history of the Knights Templar.[1] But, as a devout Catholic, there is another reason why he might have omitted the connection.

Hugh de Payen was far from being an ideal husband. In a letter dating from 1124, we find him being castigated by Ivo, Bishop of Chartres, for abandoning his wife and vowing himself to the 'Knighthood of Christ'.[2] The assumption espoused by certain contemporary authors that the Templars were anything other than a brotherhood of celibate fighting monks dedicated to the furthering of the interests of Christianity is patently nonsensical. Women played no part in their lifestyle. As a married man, and the Order's founder and leader, it would have been unthinkable for de Payen to remain with his wife, which would hardly have endeared him to her relatives.

The Knights Templar, their dramatic white capes displaying the symbolic red cross of martyrdom, arrived in Scotland in 1128, not long after they had become established in England. The Scottish king, David I, having been schooled at the court of his brother-in-law, Henry I of England, must have known of their reputation long before he inherited the Scottish throne in 1124. In an age of deep spiritual commitment, where the Knights Templar were seen as the avenging angels of Holy Rome, it was only to be expected that he should welcome them to his realm, especially if there were family ties within his immediate circle of friends. Since this circle of friends was almost entirely comprised of the knightly Norman companions he had acquired while in England, those family ties were, in every respect, considerable.

The Cistercian monk Aelred de Rievaulx went so far as to claim that the Scottish king surrounded himself with Templar advisers.[3] Certainly, there is plenty of evidence to confirm King David's willingness to support religious orders. In this, he was very much his mother's son. Around 1140, for example, he granted lands at Torphichen, in West Lothian, to the Benedictine Knights Hospitaller of the Order of St John of Jerusalem who already occupied the islands of Rhodes and Cyprus and would eventually control Malta. The remains of their preceptory at Torphichen survive to this day.

If Hugh de Payen was genuinely the brother-in-law or son-in-law of Henry St Clair, he would obviously have had ready access to the king when he arrived in Scotland on the northern leg of his British recruitment tour of 1128. In all probability, they might even have met previously in England. From the beginning, de Payen's purpose was to place his followers close to figures of power to promote the spiritual benefits of their participating in the Crusades. At the same time, he was fundraising. Profits from the

Templars' substantial agricultural and manufacturing enterprises throughout Europe were pooled to finance their wider mission.

Gifted land at Balantrodoch, 11 miles south of Edinburgh, mature Templar monks, for the most part with their Crusading days behind them, created, in 1128, a preceptory featuring a mill and simple chapel situated on a small promontory above the River South Esk. Hidden from view, yet in the midst of the lush Midlothian meadowland which flanks Edinburgh's southern approaches, this was only a brisk cross-country ride on horseback to the knightly Norman fiefdoms of the neighbouring St Clairs at Rosslyn and the Ramsays at Dalhousie; to the west, at Corstorphine, were the Forresters; to the east at Pencaitland and Luffness, the Setons. All were close friends and confidants of the king.

In a society profoundly obsessed with Crusading zeal, gifts of lands to the Templars – and Hospitallers – not only confirmed the support of the monarch, but enabled the monks to embark upon money-making ventures, the proceeds from which were put towards the greater good of the Order. Promising a great victory in the name of the Lord, Templars became business consultants, and money lenders. Travelling alone on foot or on horse was exceedingly dangerous throughout the European continent, so bodyguards were provided for pilgrims to the Holy Land. Through letters of credit, exchangeable through their various secretariats located in different countries, and with Latin as the lingua franca, they introduced the first traveller's cheques. In their commercial dealings and operational expertise, the Poor Knights were far from poor.

Today the tiny Midlothian village which sits on the summit above Balantrodoch is known as Temple and consists of a picturesque main street of cottage-style eighteenth-century dwelling houses. It is hard to imagine that it was once a recruitment centre for Christian mercenaries. And indeed the fact is that subsequent to the Templars' dispersal, between 1307 and 1309, the term 'Temple' was widely applied to any land or property previously held by them and, as is the case with neighbouring Rosslyn Chapel, their association with the ruined sixteenth-century Old Parish Church seen here today is also a diversion. Despite its Rose-Croix façade, it was actually built around three hundred years after the Templars were disbanded by the Hospitallers of St John, who, under the terms of the dissolution, had acquired their land. However, stones on the church's north wall most probably did form part of the Templars' original preceptory. And local oral tradition still hints at the existence of the Templars' mythical treasure: 'Twixt the oak and the elm tree/ You will find buried the millions free.'

The Templar community at Balantrodoch flourished for over a century. Indeed, by the late thirteenth century, the Templars had become substantial landowners in Scotland. They held 8,000 acres at Maryculter in Aberdeenshire. At Dalry, within the royal parklands of Holyrood, the farm of Orchardfield became a Templar property, as did tenement buildings within the Old Town of Edinburgh at the head of the Cowgate, in Greyfriars' Park, and on the Fore Stairs, adjoining Edinburgh Castle. In St Andrews, they owned a tenement at the Mercat Cross, and had similar properties in Aberdeen and Lanark. In his book *Reminiscences and Notices of the Parishes of the County of Haddington*, published in 1883,[4] my ancestor John Martine makes reference to a Knights Templar chapel which stood at the Custom Stone, where four streets diverged. He also refers to their 800 acres of rich farmland at Drem.

Already wealthy from patronage the length and breadth of Europe, the Templars must have believed themselves invincible. However, in 1291 their Master of Scotland, Brian de Jay, swore fealty to Edward I of England and, in doing so, undermined the Order's code of neutrality.[5] Renowned as an opportunist and villain, de Jay was to inspire the fictional Sir Brian de Bois-Guilbert of Sir Walter Scott's novel *Ivanhoe*. His death fighting against the Scots at the Battle of Falkirk in 1298 allowed his successors to adopt a more independent stance, but far too much has been read into this independence. In any squabble between secular leaders, the Templars' allegiance was inalienably to the Pope. In this way they were expected to remain indifferent to confrontations such as those that took place between England and France, and, in the late thirteenth century, between Scotland and England. The Templar's ultimate crime was that, with their widespread accumulated wealth, commanderies and castles from Cyprus to the Baltic, they were seen by some as being just a little bit too invincible.

All of Christendom shuddered when, on Friday 13 October, 1307 (a day and a date thereafter associated with ill fortune), with the full support of Pope Clement V, the French king, Philip IV, ordered the arrest of all Templar brothers in France, charging them with an entire catalogue of heresy which encompassed the denial of Christ, sodomy, cat worship, the veneration of a skull, and excessive secrecy.[6] But the story goes that some of their number were forewarned and that Templar ships anchored at La Rochelle immediately set out to sea; some to Portugal, the remainder to Scotland to seek sanctuary from the Scottish king. This made sense since the previous year Robert the Bruce, having been implicated in the murder of his cousin, John 'the Red' Comyn, had himself been excommunicated by Pope Clement.

A Ban of Excommunication was among the worst fates that could befall a king. It was a political tool directed at the individual, but if it was interpreted literally it applied to the kingdom as well. In an age of deeply held faith, it was ferocious. The effect upon the mediaeval mind can only be likened to the early response to the spread of Aids. Mercifully, no television or tabloid press existed to tell the general public of the fourteenth century that they were denied salvation, and that all of their children would be stigmatised as bastards. Still, it was a fearful indictment and, as a result, excommunicated kings could find themselves with a lot on their consciences! The celebration of Mass was forbidden. Marriages could not be held in a church, and the dead were denied burial in Holy Ground, hence the mediaeval invention of those pretty little lych-gates upon the boundaries of episcopal terrain, being the nearest anyone could get to God during times of excommunication and plague.

The consequence, however, was that Scotland emerged as the only place in Europe where Papal Law was ignored and could not be vigorously enforced. Thus, the fugitive Templars, as distinct from their brotherhood who were already established in the country, are believed to have set up a headquarters at Kilmartin, a sheltered glen close to the ancient Scottish coronation site of Dunadd, in Argyll. Grave slabs dating from the late thirteenth and early fourteenth century and featuring knightly figures and Templar crosses can still be seen in the churchyard.

Since their escape route was from northern France, the Templar refugees would have avoided the main trade routes of the English Channel and Irish Sea to circumnavigate the west coast of Ireland, bringing them through the Firth of Lorne to the Mull of Kintyre where Bruce's great ally Angus Og of Clan Donald was all-powerful. At Kilmartin, the Templars' significant military skills were soon put to good use in manufacturing weapons and training up recruits for the Scots army. The full implications of their location would become evident seven years later.

The arrest, interrogation, torture and burning of Templars in Paris and elsewhere in France continued relentlessly until 18 March 1314, when the Grand Master Jacques de Molay and the Commander of Normandy, Geoffrey de Charney, were fed to the flames on an island in the River Seine. Within five weeks, Pope Clement V, their tormentor, was also dead. Two months later, the Scottish and English armies faced one another across the marshland of the Bannock Burn below Stirling Castle. Robert the Bruce's triumph on 24 June changed everything so far as Scotland was concerned, and indeed, the Scottish Templars, it is claimed, provided the unidentified supplementary force which appeared as from nowhere to put the English to flight.

A new era had begun, and Bruce, securely established upon the Scottish throne, desperately needed the sanction and support of

Christendom. It would therefore have been impolitic to be seen as the protector of a proscribed band of heretics, regardless of the unfairness of that judgement. The 11th Earl of Elgin, whose family descend from the same Bruce line as King Robert, and who for four years during the 1960s served as Grand Master Mason of Scotland, observed, when I asked him, that his kinsman always seems to have remained passive about the Templars. 'He certainly permitted them to hold land and presumably to continue to recruit,' he said. 'In practical terms they possibly were suppliers of much of his armoury, sword blades and so forth.'

Andrew Sinclair in *Rosslyn: The Story of Rosslyn Chapel and the True Story Behind* The Da Vinci Code (Birlinn, 2005) is convinced that this is the case. With weaponry in constant demand, they definitely had the expertise and, in the years running up to their dispersal, the necessary forges and blacksmiths at their disposal. But no contemporary confirmation exists and this is only pure speculation. Both before and immediately after the Scottish victory at Bannockburn, a conspiracy of silence appears to have prevailed over anything to do with the Templars' activities in Scotland. Or was it simply that no one was interested? That seems unlikely, but it was probably considered best to remain silent by all concerned.

Throughout Europe, all Templar allegiances were redistributed. Their properties were either reallocated to the Order of the Hospital of St John of Jerusalem, a more passive Christian brotherhood dedicated to the relief of sickness, or returned to the landowning families who had originally gifted them. In Portugal, a new Military Order, the Order of Christ, was created, and in Valencia – otherwise known as the Kingdom of Aragon – the Order of Montesa was set up.[7] Only a handful of the Order's leaders in England and Ireland were rounded up and brought to trial, more as a gesture towards Rome than anything else. At the same time, Edward II of England, who had succeeded his father only three months before the Papal decree of 1307, took it upon himself to issue an order for the arrest of all Templars in Scotland.

This had little effect as by then his influence north of the Border was dwindling fast. And the question has to be asked, were there any Templars still around to be arrested?

Two elderly knights, Walter de Clifton, the Preceptor at Balantrodoch, and William de Middleton, were successfully rounded up, and a third, Thomas Tocci, voluntarily surrendered. All three were brought before William Lamberton, Bishop of St Andrews, and prosecuted by John Solario, the Papal Legate in Scotland.[8] Among those who gave evidence against them were Sir Henry St Clair of Rosslyn, great-great-great-grandson of the Crusader Henry, and his son William, which tends to suggest that by this stage the knightly St Clairs had seriously distanced themselves from the Order.

After what amounted to little more than a show trial, de Clifton, de Middleton and Tocci were found not guilty and sent to Cistercian monasteries in the Scottish Borders. This was the final denouement of the Order of the Poor Knights of the Temple of Solomon in Scotland. Under Papal decree, Balantrodoch and Maryculter were acquired by the Benedictine Order of Knights Hospitallers, and the assumption is that those Templar monks who remained simply swapped their white habits for the black of the Hospitallers. Others may have chosen anonymity and, in so doing, in line with popular fiction, laid the seeds for their descendants to re-emerge three hundred years later posing as Scottish Freemasons (see Chapter 10).

On the Internet there are currently in the region of 1,470,000 websites connected with the Knights Templar scattered around the globe. These include: the Grand Encampment of Knights Templar of the United States, based in Bellaire; the New Order of the Knights Templar and Daughters of Tsion (The Ladies Templar); the Ordo Supremus Militaris Templi Hierosolymitani Knights Templar; the Magistral Grand Priory of the Holy Lands (a UK-based charity); and the International Order of Knights Templar, Ordo Supremus Militaris Hiersolymilitani (Sovereign Order of the Temple of Jerusalem), founded in 1854, claiming more than 5,000 members and special consultative status to the United Nations – granted in July 2001.

Militi Templi Scotia (MTS) is the oldest Order of the Temple active in Scotland and traces its origins to the reformation of the Templar order in Scotland in 1789 under Alexander Deuchar, who revitalised it after the death of Prince Charles Edward Stuart the last master of the old, Masonic, Order. Stipulating that it is of Christian and 'Non-Masonic' origin, its members adopt many of the moral and ethical stances of the original Christian order.

However, none of these modern membership organisations have any plausible ancestral link with the twelfth-century creation of Hugh de Payen. They are the stuff of romantic fiction. Similarly, and equally surrounded by mysteries of its own self-indulgent invention, is the shadowy Prieuré de Sion which features so significantly in both *The Holy Blood and The Holy Grail* and *The Da Vinci Code*. Credited with being the secret Catholic control centre behind the Knights Templar, there are an equally amazing 85,400 websites associated with this subject. Said to have been founded as early as 1099, but in all likelihood a twentieth-century invention, its provenance is examined in Chapter 16.

✠

FIVE

The Battle of Roslin Glen

Scotland's Wars of Independence

On the night of 24 February 1303 the first castle at Rosslyn, which certainly dated from the eleventh century and probably stood on the site of today's chapel (see Chapter 6), found itself at the very heart of the struggle for Scottish independence. In the space of the following twenty-four hours, a Scottish force of 8,000 men overwhelmed and defeated an English army of 30,000 in three bloody encounters. The first confrontation took place in the parkland immediately south-west of where the castle then stood; the second, in the Kilburn area of the neighbouring Dryden estate to the north. With the third attack, it was an English wipe-out. For Scotland it was payback time.

After his defeat and capture at the first Battle of Dunbar seven years earlier, Henry St Clair, 7th Baron – along with his brother William, his son William, as well as his kinsmen John St Clair of Herdmanston, and a Gregory St Clair – was among the 2,000 Scottish landowners, churchmen and burgesses who swore allegiance to Edward I of England at Berwick.[1] They had had little option but to sign. Not without reason did Edward I become known as the 'Hammer of the Scots'. A brilliant soldier and military strategist, he was unquestionably also a psychopath. The fate that he later decreed for Sir William Wallace, who was courageous enough to defy him, was totally repugnant. Wallace was hanged until almost dead, drawn (in other words disembowelled) and quartered (cut in four). His body parts were placed on public display thereafter. This was the penalty for treason in England, first introduced by Edward himself. Wallace's contemporary, Dafydd ap Gruffydd, the Welsh freedom fighter, brother of Llywelyn, Prince of Wales, suffered a similar fate. What makes it so particularly unforgivable in these cases is that Wallace was a Scot, and Gruffydd, Welsh. They were therefore prisoners-of-war, not traitors.

Following the Battle of Dunbar, the tyrant Edward's army swarmed across Scotland like a plague of wasps, as far north as the Moray Firth, capturing castles and confiscating the Stone of Destiny and Holy Rude, the paramount symbols of Scotland's divinity. His soldiers even seized all of the National Archives of Scotland, an act tantamount to mediaeval genocide. In the tradition of revisionist politicians throughout time, the English king was intent on rubbing out the past. For the majority of Scotland's nobility, however, there were too many vested interests at stake to stand up to him: many of them, including Robert the Bruce's family, had extensive land interests in England. They could, and did, bide their time.

Meanwhile, having fortified the coastal town of Berwick, King Edward returned to London leaving Sir John de Segrave behind as his Governor of Scotland and Commander of Edinburgh Castle. While Edward became increasingly preoccupied with France, and in subjugating the Welsh, Sir John, basing himself in Carlisle, set about systematically subduing the various pockets of defiance north of the Scottish border.

Lechery and innocence sell a story, and creative minds would have us believe that the English offensive against Roslin was of a distinctly personal nature; in other words, that a woman was involved. Certainly it makes for a good yarn, although no contemporary evidence exists to substantiate it. We are told, however, that Sir John, incidentally a married man, had become enamoured of Lady Margaret Ramsay, sister of Sir William Ramsay of Dalhousie, an estate that lies less than 5 miles from

Roslin, at Bonnyrigg. Lady Margaret, for her part, apparently had her eye on the son of Sir Henry St Clair, 7th Lord of Rosslyn, and when news of their impending marriage reached Sir John, he reacted with vigour, determined to put an end to the nuptials.

Whether there is any truth in this story or not, he certainly did arrive in the town of Melrose, and divided his men into three equal divisions. His deputy, Sir Robert Neville, was sent to attack Borthwick Castle, near Fushiebridge, which was being held by Sir Gilbert Hay. A force under Sir Ralph Confrey was sent to secure Dalhousie Castle, while the remaining army, under Sir John, assisted by Ralph de Manton, the English paymaster, marched on Rosslyn Castle.[2] Their timing could not have been worse. First, Sir John's men were surrounded by the advancing Scots, who charged into them in the darkness. On the far side of the castle promontory, the Scots then formed a battle line and the English division approaching from the north was met with a volley of arrows forcing it to swerve towards a steep ravine with the river below. The conclusion that followed was fast and violent. The Scots, who knew their territory well, took up a position at the top of the ravine and pushed the English into the gorge where their ranks were rapidly decimated.

In 1994, a commemorative cairn was erected by Roslin Heritage Society on the spot now known as Mountmarle. The story goes that as the English were fleeing, one of their number called out to one of their leaders, a member of the Anglo-Norman de Marle family, 'Mount, Marle and ride!'[3] Another legend tells of a phantom hound, whose eerie baying can still be heard in the woods on stormy nights. During the fighting a large war dog, owned by an English knight, viciously attacked the Scottish soldier who had killed his master and was struck to the ground. Later that night, the beast was seen prowling in the castle guardroom. Over the following weeks, the 'Mauthe Doog', 'dog of darkness' as it became known, haunted the soldier to death.[4]

In command of the Scottish army were Henry St Clair, Sir

Symon Fraser of Neidpath Castle, near Peebles, and John Comyn, Earl of Buchan, generally known as the 'Red Comyn', the same Red Comyn who, three years later, almost to the day, would die during a violent confrontation at Dumfries with his kinsman, Robert the Bruce. Also present on the battlefield were Sir Simon of the Lee, Somerfield of Carnwath, and Fleming of Cumbernauld.

Sir William Wallace, appointed Guardian of Scotland in the name of the deposed king, John Balliol, had been expected to lead the attack, but had declined, still raw from his defeat at the Battle of Falkirk five years earlier. Most of what we know of Wallace comes from the words of Henry the Minstrel, or Blind Harry as he is more commonly known, who composed his Scottish propaganda epic *The Life and Heroic Actions of Sir William Wallace, General and Governor of Scotland* a century and a half after the guerrilla leader was betrayed, captured and then brutally dismembered in the streets of London. It is, nevertheless, generally accepted among academic circles that Blind Harry's epic polemic was fuelled rather more by the poet's personal anti-English prejudices than by fact. The narrative is therefore much exaggerated, and, similarly, the Australian actor Mel Gibson's 1995 film *Braveheart*, while fuelling the fires of Scottish nationalism, does historical accuracy no favours.

As regards the Battle of Roslin, all the available evidence suggests that William Wallace was in France at the time, although a cave in the cliffs of Hawthornden, where he is alleged to have taken shelter at some stage during his adventures, carries his name, as we have already seen. Scotland's future king, the 29-year-old Robert the Bruce, was certainly in Ireland at the time and was not, at this stage, committed in the developing conflict. The glory for the Scots' victory on this occasion must unquestionably go to Comyn, Fraser and St Clair.

And to yet another, lesser-known, individual. It is on record that the Scottish army was alerted to the approaching danger by Prior Abernethy of a Cistercian priory located close to Roslin.

Unfortunately, this poses yet another historical conundrum since the nearest Cistercian priory to Roslin was at Newbattle, south of Dalkeith – the nearest Cistercian abbey being at Melrose. Prior Abernethy, it transpires, had previously been a Knight Templar, thus giving the lie to the assertion that religious orders did not take sides.[5]

With both orders dating from the eleventh century, the Cistercians and Knights Templar, despite the former retaining a vow of silence, were so closely linked through ties of blood, patronage and shared objectives that many scholars consider them to be one and the same. Added to this, it is highly improbable that the Templar preceptory at Balantrodoch would have remained untouched by the invasion. And it is equally unlikely, despite the Templars' professed code of impartiality, that they would have turned their backs on the plight of the St Clair family with whom they had been so closely aligned since their beginning.

With the absence of primary historical leaders, the Battle of Roslin is not nearly as well known as Wallace's victory at Stirling Bridge six years earlier or Bruce's triumph at Bannockburn eleven years later. It was nevertheless equally as bloody as both, if not more so, as names around the village testify: Shinbones Field, where bones of the dead continue to be unearthed; the Hewan, where a burial mound remains; and the Stinking Rig, where the smell of decomposing corpses lingered on for decades. Tradition has it that the Kilburn, a rivulet which runs off the North Esk, ran red with blood for three days following the carnage. In the aftermath of the battle, therefore, in gratitude for their victory, each survivor carried a stone to the summit of the hill where a cairn was formed to serve as an altar. Appropriately, this hill was already known as the Carnethy, the 'hill of the cairn'. Although superseded by more momentous and headline-grabbing events, it could certainly be argued that without the confidence-boost that their triumph at the Battle of Roslin brought to Scotland's freedom fighters, Scotland's Wars of Independence might not have continued. Now, the die was cast.

In the aftermath of the conflict, Sir John de Segrave and Ralph de Manton were taken prisoner and richly ransomed. William St Clair married Lady Margaret Ramsay, and over the following twenty-five years, before Scotland's independence was finally accepted by the English with the signing of the Treaty of Northampton in 1328, England's overlordship was severely tested. Moreover, between 25 and 26 March 1306, in a supreme act of defiance, Robert the Bruce was inaugurated as Sovereign of Scotland at Scone Abbey. In the absence of the Stone of Destiny, the ritual coronation seat of Scotland, such ceremonial as there was followed an even more ancient tradition. The High Sennachie of Scotland, the official royal genealogist, a position today occupied by the Lord Lyon King of Arms, would have read out the Bruce royal pedigree reaching far back into the mists of time through the marriage of his great-grandfather to the great-grand-daughter of David I, and the citation would have culminated with a resounding cheer from his supporters. Despite the fact that it had become common practice among European monarchs, however, there was no anointment with holy oil to bring him into line with the king of England, as an anointed sovereign. In mediaeval Europe, the anointment of a ruler with holy oil transferred divine right to its recipient, and those anointed became *Dei Gratia*, 'by the grace of God'. Only the Pope in Rome was in a position to sanction such an entitlement, and, along with the lifting of his second excommunication, it was finally granted to King Robert by Pope John XXII literally months before his death, and then only on the receipt of a substantial sum of money. Nor was a countess of Buchan, as is widely claimed, on hand on the first day to crown him. This is a fiction created at a later stage to add romance to the occasion.

In the ancient hierarchy of Scotland, the earls of Fife were traditionally given the responsibility for placing the crown of Scotland on the heads of Scottish kings. The story goes that since Bruce was implicated in the murder of his kinsman and friend John Comyn, Duncan, Earl of Fife, refused to have anything to do with him. Duncan's sister Isabella, Countess of Buchan, however, not an admirer of Comyn, is said to have volunteered to step into the breach instead and allegedly crowned Bruce on the second day of the inauguration ceremonies, more as a theatrical gesture than as part of the official ritual. The 11th Earl of Elgin, from whose family King Robert descended, agrees that the actual ceremony, surrounded by uncertainty and in the absence of the Stone of Destiny, would have been a modest occasion with a minimum of fuss. However, as punishment for the countess's action, King Edward I of England is reputed to have taken her hostage and imprisoned her in a cage hung from the walls of Berwick Castle.

In the absence of Scotland's reliquaries of the Roman religion, notably the Holy Rude, the artefacts of Dalriada's old Celtic religion were reinstated: the Pastoral Staff of St Moluag, a sixth-century Irish Pictish monk; and the Monymusk Reliquary, a bejewelled casket covered in bronze and silver plates, and said to contain the bones of St Columba of Iona, the Irish missionary who had reintroduced Christianity to Scotland during the Dark Ages. The latter was to be paraded before the Scottish army immediately before the Battle of Bannockburn.[6] Today, custody of the Pastoral Staff is entrusted to the Livingstone family, who became almoners to Lismore Cathedral and barons of Bachuil on the island of Lismore, off mainland Argyll. A Latin charter of 1544, still held by the family, confirms immemorial possession of their lands and such possessions as survive of St Moluag. The Lyon Court, being the ultimate authority on matters relating to the Scottish Crown, in 1950 declared that the staff's custodian is the co-arbiter of St Moluag and a baron in the Baronage of Argyll and the Isles, thus confirming the original Latin Charter. The Monymusk Reliquary can be seen in the National Museum of Scotland in Edinburgh.

There is no accurate reportage of what took place at Scone on that day in March seven centuries ago, but since Sir Henry St Clair and his sons John and William were among Robert the Bruce's most loyal supporters, it is only to be assumed that they were in attendance. Edward I of England died the following year and his dying wish was that the war be continued. And therefore Sir Henry and his sons certainly fought alongside Sir Henry's brother, the Bishop of Dunkeld, and their kinsman, Sir William St Clair of Herdmanston, at the confrontation which took place eight years later on Midsummer's Day beside the Bannock Burn, near Stirling. Sir Henry's reward was the Barony of Pentland, which had last been held by his great-great-grandfather. In further gratitude, King Robert rewarded Herdmanston with a sword which he had inscribed '*Le Roi me donne St Cler me porte*', 'The King gave me, St Clair wields me.'

This sword is not to be confused with the four-handed, 5-foot long Great Sword of Bruce, which is in the possession of the 11th earl of Elgin. Another sword – a Claymore with four 'quillons', or cross-guards on the handle, and previously kept at Hawthornden, but now housed with the National Museum of Scotland – also makes a claim to be Bruce's sword, but this is unlikely since its appearance is undoubtedly sixteenth century.

After Bannockburn there followed a temporary respite for the Scots, which to some extent enabled them to lead a more leisured existence. Like most of his contemporaries, King Robert's favourite pastime was hunting, and on one royal excursion into the Pentland Hills, he challenged his nobles that their hounds would be unable to catch a particular white deer he had seen on a previous occasion. The rash William St Clair immediately wagered his head that his two hounds, Help and Hold, would kill the deer before it reached the March Burn, and the bet was on.[7] Fortunately, Help and Hold caught the deer and William kept his head.

The war between Scotland and England dragged on with sporadic skirmishes for another fourteen years. In addition to an incursion on the Fife coast in 1317 – a landing successfully repelled by Sir Henry's brother, Bishop William St Clair – Edward II of England persisted with a series of intermittent Border raids and, naturally, Rosslyn Castle was continually in the front line of defence. One of Sir Henry St Clair's neighbours, Sir Alexander Ramsay, is an all but forgotten hero of this turbulent age.

Appointed Warden of the Middle Marches, he used the crags and caves of Gorton and Hawthornden as a base for his band of guerrilla fighters to intercept the convoys of the enemy, capture their provisions and seriously hinder their operations. Were Roslin Glen then a lochan, their hiding place in the cliffs would have been all but invisible. They were brave, resourceful men, these Norman-Scots, and defiant to the end. No Anglo-Norman was allowed to get the better of them. In 1319, exasperated at his inability to tame the Scots, Edward II, like his father before him, urged the pope, now John XXII, successor to Clement V, to once again excommunicate the Scottish king, which he duly did.

Enough was enough. Such blatant hypocrisy did the Church no favours. On 6 April 1320, Henry St Clair of Rosslyn and his cousins, including Magnus St Clair of Caithness and Sir Alexander Ramsay of Dalhousie, were among the signatories of the Declaration of Arbroath, which collectively entreated the pope to legitimise Robert the Bruce as their rightful sovereign. In May 1328, both Pope John XXII and the English king, now the sixteen-year-old Edward III, finally relented. A treaty was signed at Northampton, but the following June King Robert died at Cardross, in Dunbartonshire.

A devout Christian, morally undermined by his two excommunications and haunted by the murder of his cousin, the Red Comyn, it had been his lifelong, but unspoken, ambition to make peace with his god by participating in a pilgrimage to the Holy Land. He left instructions to that effect, but considered in retrospect, and even now, it seems an extraordinary and rather gruesome undertaking. The king's body was interred in Dunfermline Abbey, and, soon afterwards, a group of Scottish knights, comprising some of his closest supporters during his lifetime, set sail from the Firth of Forth en route for Jerusalem carrying with them his embalmed heart encased in a conical casket. Sir Henry

St Clair, by then too old to travel, sent his sons William and John in his place. Accompanying the St Clairs and Sir James 'the Good' Douglas, Bruce's closest friend, and the group's leader, were Simon Locard of the Lee, Robert and Walter Logan of Restalrig and William Keith of Calton.

Southern Spain was scheduled as a last port of call before crossing the Mediterranean. However, when the party of knights arrived in Seville, it was soon sidetracked and rapidly became embroiled in the on-going conflict between King Alfonso XI of Castile and Leon, and the Moors, the Muslim inhabitants of Al-Andalus, otherwise known as Andalusia.

In fairness, the Moors had occupied this territory for nearly half a millennium, but the small town of Teba de Ardales in Andalusia was now under siege by King Alfonso's soldiers, and Douglas, imbued with Crusader zeal, and sparring for a fight, impetuously offered his support. Emotions ran high, and in the heat of the ensuing battle against the Infidel, Sir James Douglas recklessly charged into the fray with the casket containing King Robert's heart strung around his neck. Finding himself surrounded, the old warrior, realising his time was up, impetuously hurled the container in front of him, crying out 'Now pass on, as ever was thy wont in life, first in the fight, and Douglas will follow thee or die!'

Both of the St Clair brothers, and both Logan brothers, fell with their leader, but the casket was rescued by Keith and Locard, whose family at some later stage changed their surname to Lockhart.[8] The Moors, impressed by the bravery of the Scots, allowed the survivors to go free and to retrieve the bodies of their compatriots. The casket containing Bruce's heart was also re-turned to Scotland and sent to Melrose Abbey, where his son, David II, gave instructions for it to be buried in front of the altar.

No one had ever doubted that this interment took place, but it was still rather miraculous when, during archaeological investiga-tions in 1996, a small conical casket about 10 inches high by 4 inches in diameter at its base, tapering to a flat lid at the top about

1 ½ inches across, was discovered. Although worn with age, the inscription was still legible: 'The enclosed leaden casket containing a heart was found beneath Chapter House floor, March 1921, by His Majesty's Office of Works.' The casket containing the heart was not reopened on this occasion, but was buried again during a private ceremony at Melrose Abbey on 22 June 1998. A carved red sandstone marker had been commissioned by Historic Scotland and was unveiled a few days later by the then Secretary of State for Scotland, Donald Dewar, on the anniversary of the Battle of Bannockburn.

Following the Battle of Teba, the remains of William and John St Clair were taken to Rosslyn, but as the chapel did not then exist, it can only be assumed that they were interred in the old cemetery situated lower down the hill.

⚜

SIX

The Castle of Rosslyn

Sentinel of the Lothians

Father Hay tells us that, according to the oral tradition of the St Clairs, following the Scottish victory at Roslin in February 1303, an English prisoner, 'a man of no small estimation', whom Sir Henry St Clair had taken prisoner and befriended, sought to counsel him concerning the vulnerability of his existing castle and suggested that he build a fortification on the rock upon which the current castle now stands.[1] The temptation is to assume that this was either a repentant Sir John de Segrave, seeking to make amends for his previous interest in Sir Henry's daughter-in-law, Lady Margaret, or Ralph de Manton.

Whoever it was, the advice was taken sufficiently seriously by Sir Henry for him to make a decision to relocate his stronghold. This inevitably raises the question of where the original castle might have stood, and although it has been suggested that it guarded the south bank of the river, or lochan, of Roslin Glen, a more obvious conclusion, endorsed by the complexity of its foundations, is that the earlier fortification occupied the present-day site of the chapel, high on the hill, where it commanded extensive views of the surrounding countryside but was open to attack on all sides.

It seems odd at first that the chosen spot for the St Clairs' new build should have been on the lower ground, below the hilltop fastness, but it would not have been at all ill-advised were there water surrounding it. The tower of the present castle of Rosslyn, the earliest surviving piece of masonry on this site, is dated from around the year 1340, which approximately confirms the time-scale involved. The availability of a large quantity of locally quarried sandstone was an obvious bonus. Mediaeval castles needed to be impregnable, but many buildings were still fabricated of wood as, for example, was the greater part of Edinburgh Castle when its English occupants were attacked by Bruce's lieutenant, the Earl of Moray, in 1314. Remember that this was the age of the longbow, footsoldiers carrying pikes and spears, and mounted cavalry attacks. Siege artillery, such as trebuchets and catapults, was only just being developed and proved no serious threat until well into the following century.

Effective siege weaponry, employing gunpowder and necessitating a widespread change to building in stone, only began to emerge in the mid fifteenth century with huge guns capable of hurling stones weighing as much as 350 kilograms over a distance of 2.5 miles. In 1457, James II of Scotland was presented with two massive siege guns by Philip the Good, Duke of Burgundy, his uncle by marriage. The surviving cannon is known as Mons Meg, having been tested during an assault on the Belgian town of Mons, close to the French border, and it is housed in Edinburgh Castle. The unfortunate James was perhaps rather too keen on his artillery. He was killed in 1460 when another of his guns exploded during the siege of Roxburgh Castle.

In working out the layout of a building that has been repeatedly assaulted and rebuilt over the centuries, the use of imagination is essential. There are nine steps cut into the rock below the high wall of Rosslyn Castle. These adjoin the Lamp Tower, which possibly led to the terrace above. The information that has been passed down to us by Father Hay is that the approach pathway to the drawbridge was known as Minstrels Walk, commemorating a long-vanished house that once accommodated Prince William's harpers and minstrels. And that is all we really know of the original layout.

The new castle at Rosslyn came under minor attack on many occasions. Edward III of England invaded Scotland on four separate forays between 1334 and 1337, during which time the majority of Lowland Scots decamped into the hills to get out of his way. While this was going on, William St Clair, 8th Baron of Rosslyn, had taken himself off to Lithuania on a Crusade with the Teutonic Knights, who shared a similar purpose with the Templars, only in their case it was to purge the pagans of north-eastern Europe. In 1369, however, a twenty-five year truce between England and Scotland was negotiated. The lord of Rosslyn Castle at this time, Henry, 1st St Clair Prince of Orkney, who succeeded to his father's estates in 1358, was to be found principally in the far north, in Orkney, where he was building Kirkwall Castle, and thereafter on his travels abroad.[2] During his theoretical transatlantic excursion (see Chapter 7), he would have been absent for over eleven years, so it was left to his son, also Henry, to make improvements to Rosslyn Castle. However, this must have been delayed by Henry junior's capture and imprisonment in England, for reasons which will soon become clear.

Almost his first action on being released in 1407 was to supervise the building of Rosslyn's great dungeon. If the second Prince Henry learned anything from the murder of his pioneering father at Kirkwall in 1400, it was to secure his surroundings. He placed the five-storey-high, fifty-foot-long entrance to the main dwelling on the far side of the inner courtyard. It was these levels which gave the castle its lofty and unassailable appearance. In mediaeval Scotland, a family such as St Clair needed to awe their enemies in order to keep them at a distance.

The 2nd Prince Henry of Orkney had, in 1406, been appointed guardian of the future James I by King Robert III, who was only too aware of his approaching mortality and the avarice of his brother, the Duke of Albany. The strategy was for them to go abroad where James would be safe from the machinations of the Scottish nobility. The royal party embarked for France, but, in the words of Father Hay, 'Prince James not being able to abide the smell of the waters, desired to be at land, where when they were come (for they landed at his request upon the coast of England), upon their journey to the King, they were taken and imprisoned'.[3]

The young prince having fallen so effortlessly into his clutches, Henry IV of England decided to hold on to him, 'yet so he caused instructors to teach Prince James, where through he became so learned and expert in all things, that he had no equal'. Back in Scotland, alas, the news of his son's capture brought on King Robert's rapid demise. As for Henry St Clair, it was hardly his fault. The landing had been on the prince's insistence, and Father Hay tells an intriguing tale.

So beloved was Prince Henry, according to the cleric, that the year after his capture, one of his Pentland tenants, John Johnstone, set off for England intent on rescuing him. Having arrived at the prison where his landlord was incarcerated, he played the fool so cunningly that, without arousing suspicion as to who he might be, he gained entrance. Winning the confidence of the jailers, he one night managed to extricate Henry St Clair from his confinement and, accompanying him to the gate heavily disguised, the two of them escaped under cover of darkness.[4]

The return home, however, was not so joyous as might have been expected. The Duke of Albany, by then Governor of Scotland, accused the Lord of Rosslyn of treason for having allowed his nephew to be taken prisoner by the English. Fortunately, Albany's widespread unpopularity worked in St Clair's favour. When the former arrived to arrest him and to take possession of his lands, he found himself vastly outnumbered by Henry's followers. The duke fled to Falkland Palace in Fife, where he remained indoors until an amicable settlement was negotiated which absolved St Clair of all blame.

In 1420 the succession of William, 3rd St Clair Prince of Orkney breathed new life into Rosslyn Castle with a spate of renovation work, including the creation of a bridge under the castle and further fortification of the walls. The greater part of the north-west wall remains, with buttresses to strengthen the height, but of the other portions, only massive chunks survive. In 1893, the Revd John Thompson, the priest at St Matthews, commented on the series of openings between the rounds, or curtain walls, which resemble windows reaching near to the ground. 'Some have suggested that they were embrasures for cannon. But this is absurd on the face of it: their size and form preclude the notion, besides the fact that there was a high screen wall on the outside.'[5]

His contemporary, Andrew Kerr, was of the opinion that they were simply for the letting in of air and light into the lower apartments which, he observed, 'may have occasionally been used for keeping cattle when they could not readily be got from without; and in that case the windows or openings would be used for admitting air, and communicating with the area within the screen walls for feeding purposes'. Revd Thompson, however, dismisses Kerr's theory and says that he has not the slightest doubt that this lower apartment featuring the windows in question was the St Clair family's original private chapel within the castle walls.

Around 1447, however, as the foundations of the new chapel were in the process of being laid, disaster struck. In Father Hay's version, Edward St Clair of Dryden, arriving at Rosslyn with his greyhounds for a hunt, encountered a river of rats on the approach roads with, in their midst, a blind rat with a straw in its mouth. This, insists Father Hay, was an omen.

Prince William's first wife, the Princess Margaret, 'took great delight in little dogs and caused one of her gentlewomen to go under a bed with a lighted candle to bring forth one of them which had given birth to puppies'. Not being particularly careful, the foolish maidservant set fire to the bed, whereupon the flames spread rapidly through the apartments. William St Clair was close by on College Hill when the incident occurred. On being told what had happened, his immediate preoccupation was not so much his household or his castle, but his family's records and charters. Happily, these were saved by his chaplain who scaled down a bell-rope carrying them and, needless to say, was generously rewarded for his bravery.

It was also providential that, with the construction of the chapel in progress, there were builders on hand to repair the damage. The long delays in the completion of the chapel can in all probability be explained by the skills of masons and carpenters being diverted elsewhere. Furthermore, it should be taken into account that the castle of Ravenscraig, recently acquired in exchange for the Orkney earldom, was also a work in progress. Prince William's ongoing construction bills must have been enormous; added to this, towards the end of his life, with no less than eighteen children to support, his family relationships were in serious disarray.

In 1476, he had already resigned his most important accolade, the earldom of Caithness, to his second son by his second marriage, one can only assume – as will be discussed in Chapter 8 – to prevent his eldest son from his first marriage inheriting it. That in itself seems extremely odd in an age when primogeniture was the status quo, but then we are not privy to anything concerning the eldest son William the Waster's profligacy, nor indeed to the seriousness of the offence which prompted his father to take such drastic action. Nor do we know why Oliver, the eldest son of his second marriage, was also passed over for the Caithness earldom.

In Highland and Scandinavian tradition, chiefships were often awarded on merit to the bravest and the boldest, and the younger St Clair brother, who, to confuse the situation, was also christened William, was by all accounts more of a soldier than either of his elder siblings. It was highly unusual, if not unheard of, for a father to legally transfer a great title to a younger son, even if the older son proved useless. Such an action would certainly have required the approval of the monarch. This would have been difficult enough without the added complication that William the Waster's sister was married to King James III of Scotland's brother. Prince William must have had very sound, albeit personal, reasons for deciding to divide up his inheritance.

By contrast, wealth and land could technically be dispersed at will, although the breaking up of great estates, and especially the dispersal of land, was simply not an option among old Scottish families where the eldest son was expected to inherit everything. It can only be assumed that Prince William felt that there was infinitely more than enough to go around. Father Hay says of him, 'enriched by the deaths of his wives and new marriages, he became by far the most powerful man in the Kingdom after the Kings, and indeed the rest of the nobility gave precedence to him in wealth and statesmanship'. In the next generation, the necessities of providing for such a large family would inevitably disperse this wealth and power. Such pre-eminence could never have lasted.

⚜

SEVEN

The Northern Commonwealth

North America before Christopher Columbus

*I*t is twenty years since I visited Nova Scotia, on the north-
east coast of Canada, but it feels as if it were only yesterday
that I stood on a rise overlooking Chedabucto Bay, gazing
out to sea in the direction of Scotland. I had been told that this
was where the founder of the chapel's grandfather, Prince
Henry St Clair's expedition of 1398 had landed, a full century
before the Spanish adventurer Christopher Columbus first set
foot on the South American mainland. It all seemed so logical:
across that vast sweep of water on that warm July evening was
Orkney.

I was in Estotilanda, which only came to be known as Nova
Scotia in the seventeenth century when the canny James VI of
Scotland and I of England, ever in hope of financial gain, granted
the territory to a Scottish nobleman, Sir William Alexander of
Menstrie. I had gone to Canada that summer to attend the
Antigonish Highland Games, and the Nova Scotia International
Tattoo, a military spectacle matched only by that which takes
place each August on the esplanade of Edinburgh Castle. Everywhere I looked, from the place names to the faces and the
imported Gaelic language of the West Highlands and Hebrides,
the Scots were in evidence, descendants of those early settlers and
the victims of the Highland Clearances who followed centuries
later. Yet it made absolute sense that their Viking–Scots ancestors,

followers of the St Clair princes of Orkney, had been here even long before that.

After a week of travelling the Cabot Trail, looping around the northern tip of Cape Breton, I was convinced. The St Clair dynasty of Scotland reached a zenith in the late fourteenth century when the Sir William St Clair whose father had accompanied Bruce's heart to Spain married Isabella, daughter of one of the Northern Hemisphere's wealthiest and more powerful men, Malise, 8th Earl of Strathearn, great-grandson and heir to the Viking Jarl Gilbert of Orkney. Since Malise had no male heir, his titles passed in 1369 in the Celtic tradition through the female line to his grandson, Henry St Clair, who, ten years later, was acknowledged by the rulers of both Scotland and Norway as 42nd Jarl and 1st St Clair Jarl of Orkney (thus 1st 'Earl' of Orkney), and Jarl of Shetland. In addition, as if that was not enough, he was made Lord High Admiral of Scotland, Chief Justice of Scotland, Baron of Rosslyn, Great Protector, and Keeper and Defender of the Prince of Scotland.

While it has always been fashionably but inaccurately conjectured that the St Clairs owed their substantial wealth in no small measure to their share of the apocryphal vanished treasure of the Knights Templar, this would have been as nothing compared to the vast landholdings and sizeable income which Henry St Clair now inherited from his two grandfathers. But what should also be borne in mind is that Prince Henry, as he was styled, now had divided loyalties.

In the male-line, with landholdings in Fife and Midlothian, he owed his allegiance to Scotland's Royal House of Stewart. Through his mother, he enjoyed the status of a Scandinavian potentate answerable only to the King of Norway in Bergen. His descendant Baron St Clair Bonde, whose family is eligible for peerages in both the UK and Sweden, understands the pressures. 'I am British, and therefore my allegiance is to Her Majesty the Queen and to Scotland,' he says. 'However, I must confess that when I am in Scotland and the Scots play against the Swedes in

Scotland I am inclined to support the Swedes and conversely, when I am in a similar position in Sweden, I would support the Scots.' To a very great extent, however, the duality of his situation placed Henry in a useful position to expand not only his personal horizons, but also those of the interests he served.

With the death of her husband, Haakon VI King of Norway, in 1387, Queen Margaret of Denmark, daughter of Valdemar IV of Denmark, was made protector of both countries. When the King of Sweden intervened he was firmly suppressed, and with the Union of Kalmar, signed in 1397, Norway, Denmark and Sweden accepted Margaret's great nephew, Erik of Pomerania, as their overall ruler. When Prince Henry attended King Erik's coronation that same year, he would have been well aware that the real power in Scandinavia lay with Queen Margaret, who continued to dominate the continent until her death in 1412. As magnate of the Orkney Islands, with a fleet of wooden ocean-going Cogge ships – flat-bottomed transport vessels – in the North Sea, Henry's first initiative, having instigated the building of a great castle in Kirkwall, was to bring the remote Faroe Islands into the fold on Queen Margaret's behalf. This he achieved in 1391.

The Northern Commonwealth of Norway, Denmark and Sweden had already extended its tentacles east into the Baltic, controlling parts of Finland, Germany and Estonia. The far north of Scotland and the Orkneys – the latter territories controlled by Prince Henry – provided a jumping-off point for the western and northern oceans. For generations there had been talk of fertile lands far across the Atlantic. Norse colonies have been proved to have already existed in Iceland, Greenland, Helluland (Baffin Island) and Markland (Labrador). In 1962 early Viking settlements were excavated at Cape Bauld in Newfoundland, and Blanc Sablon, on either side of the Labrador Strait, by the Norwegian explorer Helge Ingstad and his archaeologist wife, Anne Stine. Their findings confirmed the presence of a Norse colony dating from at least the fourteenth century, if not before.[1]

To have made such a voyage with the boats they had at their

disposal was entirely possible. St Brendan, an Irish missionary from Munster, is credited with having done so as early as the sixth century, although there is considerable doubt as to exactly where he might have ended up. In 1976 the adventurer Tim Severin successfully sailed a curragh from Brandon Creek on the Dingle Peninsula to Brandon Creek on the Faroes, then across the North Atlantic to Newfoundland.[2] This was more or less the same route that was said to have been taken by the Viking explorer Leif Erikson in the tenth century. Similarly, in 1991, a West Highland galley – or birlinn – called the *Aileach* was launched with money raised by Ranald MacDonald, 24th Captain of Clan Ranald, and Wallace Clark. This magnificent boat, built by three McDonald brothers in Moville, County Donegal, and crewed by six Scotsmen and six Irishmen, sailors and oarsmen, travelled the 400-mile distance from Westport in Mayo to Stornoway.[3]

Seafaring was, of course, a dangerous enterprise, but from the fourteenth century, as the desire to explore further afield increased, it became somewhat easier with the development of navigational aids and nautical expertise. Maps began to emerge, particularly from the Mediterranean region. Indeed, much of the credibility surrounding Prince Henry's enterprise of 1398 relies upon the coincidence of a Venetian voyager Nicolò Zeno being shipwrecked on the Faroe Islands. It was not Nicolò, however, who accompanied Henry to Estotilanda, but his brother Antonio, a Venetian sea captain, whom Nicolò summoned to Orkney from Venice.

The background to the Zeno family is admirably documented in Andrew Sinclair's *The Sword and The Grail: The Story of the Grail, the Templars and the True Discovery of America*.[4] Again, a lot of this is speculation, but the facts are principally drawn from existing records and charts published in Venice by Nicolò Zeno's great-great-great-grandson in 1558. This Zeno Narrative[5] is transcribed from letters sent by Nicolò and Antonio to their brother Carlo Zeno, Captain of Venice. These provide a detailed account of the brothers' first North Atlantic expedition with a 'great lord of the islands' to Greenland in 1393, and Antonio's subsequent voyage to Estotilanda five years later in the employ of Prince Henry, by which time, it would appear, Nicolò Zeno had died. The map that accompanied the account clearly indicates the locations of Norway, Scotland, Engronelant (Greenland) and Estotilanda.

When I was in Nova Scotia I was told that in the folklore of the indigenous Mik'maqs, whose descendants survive to this day, there are long-ago stories of white gods arriving from the sea on floating islands. That the occupants of these floating islands came ashore is certain as they too are commemorated in the Mik'maq tradition, and this inevitably ties in with the claims of the Zeno Narrative. There are various east-coast locations where Prince Henry's expedition, if indeed they were the white gods whom the Mik'maqs refer to, might have set up their camp.

One is at the Castle at the Cross, a mound of stone and earth which lies 17 miles from Chester, where iron tools have been found. The other is at Oak Island in the Golden River, where there is a notorious Money Pit, a hole in the ground where, should anyone attempt to explore it, a series of flood tunnels are triggered by moving stones which give access to incoming water and thereby make it impossible to progress any further.[6]

To further endorse Prince Henry's presence, I was also shown a primitive cannon of Venetian design that had been fished out of Louisburg Harbour around 1849. There were eight rings around its barrel, and a detachable breech with a handle, a design that I was informed had become obsolete when cannons of a single shaft were introduced in the fourteenth century. Of course, it might easily have been a souvenir imported in a later century, but that would not make it nearly as intriguing.

In the spring of 1398, the Scots–Norse explorers are thought to have sailed down the New England coast to what is now known as Massachusetts. Exploring inland, they came across a tributary of the Merrimack River and found their way to a location close to what is now the town of Westford. Here, on a rock face, they, or perhaps some contemporary Native American, left behind a carving of a knightly figure holding a shield and sword. Upon the shield is an armorial drawing which the late Sir Iain Moncreiffe of that Ilk, Albany Herald at the Court of the Lord Lyon King of Arms, readily identified as the arms of Clan Gunn from Caithness, who also shared Viking blood. There is nothing like leaving a carving on a rock to let posterity know without doubt that you have been there. Which brings us to the final conundrum in this chapter.

Much is made of two decorative friezes carved into the arch surrounds at Rosslyn Chapel. One would appear to represent Indian corn; the other, cacti. Both belong to the New World, and, on the instructions of Prince Henry St Clair's grandson, were depicted a good twenty years or more before the arrival of Christopher Columbus on that continent, thus introducing a strong probability that Henry St Clair was there first. That in itself is fascinating, but my attention was then drawn by the historian Henry Steuart Fotheringham to the Great Hall of Stirling Castle where, before its total restoration by Historic Scotland in 2002, almost identical corn mouldings had existed, albeit the majority weathered beyond repair.

With an exterior makeover that makes it look like a sugar-coated cake, the majority of the surviving exterior carvings, those not already totally decimated by the weather and Reformation, were sensitively reproduced, and within the hall, decorating the high plinths which support the recreated hammerbeam ceiling, can be seen a familiar motif. Similar corn head decoration is featured on the windows in the small inner courtyard beside the Regimental Museum. 'However, things that are old do get copied by new generations and become so stylised that they ultimately become something else,' observes Steuart Fotheringham.

It is generally acknowledged that James IV built the Great Hall between 1501 and 1504, but prior to this James III certainly had a hand in starting it. Building work, in an age before mechanical diggers, when everything was fabricated by hand, took time.

Whatever the actual year of its completion, it was still long before the details of Columbus's discoveries in the New World became widely known. The existence of the corn motif does suggest a common provenance with the frieze in Rosslyn Chapel, and the most obvious explanation is that it was the work of the same cooperative of stonemasons. Alternatively, the coincidence could amount to nothing more than a contemporary invention of a fertile imagination, one which became a popular image of the time. The ubiquitous egg-and-dart cornicing of the eighteenth century springs to mind.

On the supposition that his voyage across the Atlantic was a spectacular success, Sir Henry's euphoria on returning to Scotland after another long sea voyage must have been short-lived. It was to be expected that his enemies would have monitored the movements of such a renowned and politically dangerous man to find out what he was up to. This was no pleasure trip and the eyes of the Northern Hemisphere were upon him. Discounting the very real possibility of his losing all of his ships and men, or of being drowned himself, there would come a time when he had to return and render an account of himself. This would have included his plans for creating a northern commonwealth encompassing Scandinavia, Scotland, Greenland and what is now known as North America as a counterbalance to the dominance of England and the powers of continental Europe.

And then what? The knowledge that a global northern commonwealth based on trade was not just a possibility, but in the making would certainly have alarmed the nation states of Western Europe, and not least Scotland's immediate neighbour, England. And no doubt England was well aware of what Prince Henry St Clair and the Scots had in mind. After deposing his cousin Richard II, the recently crowned Henry IV of England wasted no time in turning his army on Scotland and laying siege to Edinburgh Castle where he remained entrenched until lack of food and supplies obliged him to retreat.

With his feet firmly planted in two spheres of influence, and the potential for a third in prospect, Prince Henry posed a real threat and his enemies knew that they had to act fast. In 1400 he would pay the price of his gamesmanship. There are varying accounts of Prince Henry's death. However, the consensus was that he died when his castle in Kirkwall was attacked by raiders from East Anglia, and few were in doubt that it was a politically motivated assassination.

Prince Henry, 42nd Jarl of Orkney and 9th Lord of Rosslyn, left two sons, Henry and John, and nine daughters. Through their marriages they would make the 2nd Prince Henry St Clair one of the best-connected men in Scotland, second only to those of the Royal House of Stewart. Prince Henry's eldest sister became Countess of Douglas; the second, Countess of Dalhousie; the third, Lady Calder; the fourth, Lady Corstorphine; the fifth, Countess of Errol; the sixth, Lady Tweedie of Drumelzier; the seventh, Lady Cockburn, the Lady of Stirling; the eighth, Lady Herring, the Lady of Maretone; and the youngest, Lady Sommerville. Henry himself married a granddaughter of Archibald, Earl of Douglas and Lord of Galloway, and, through marriage, his eldest daughter became Countess of March.[7] In an age of landowning power, it is impossible to ignore the full potency of such connections. With Henry's succession in 1400, followed in 1420 by his son William, the builder of Rosslyn Chapel, the tentacles of wealth and influence of the St Clair dynasty were beyond equal in fifteenth-century Scotland.

✠

EIGHT

The Creation of Rosslyn Chapel

Vision of a Renaissance man

*B*uilding work on Rosslyn Chapel began 139 years after the Order of the Knights Templar was officially destroyed, so it is only a popular fiction which claims that it was they who built it, or, indeed, that they had anything to do with it. Of course, this is not to say that descendants of the survivors of the 1307 purge, or those who sought to maintain the movement in secrecy, might not have had a hand in it, but at no point in his history of the St Clairs of Rosslyn does Father Hay make even passing reference to the Templars. This might be explained by his having been a devout Catholic, and therefore contemptuous of the Order, but given the importance of historical clarity to him, I think it unlikely.

Realistically, Rosslyn's association with an ancient order of ritual-obsessed fighting monks has been the invention of contemporary fantasists in search of some kind of alternative Arthurian dream. Given the extraordinary array of images that were created in his chapel, it can be assumed that Prince William St Clair was himself such a fantasist, but to suggest that he was in league with the Templars is ludicrous. During his lifetime, the Templars existed only in legend, along the lines of King Arthur and Knights of the Round Table or Robin Hood. Rosslyn Chapel certainly contains genuine Templar symbolism, but what would anyone expect from the inventive imagination of its erudite patron, a man steeped in the folklore of northern Europe and beyond?

With all the focus on Rosslyn it is easy to think that it was the only church under construction at the time, and that the reasons for its inception must be similarly unique. On the contrary, the building of such places of worship was commonplace among the nobility during the fifteenth century. The Collegiate Church of the Holy Trinity, for example, was founded by Royal Charter in 1462 at Leith Wynd by Queen Mary, the widow of James II. Some of the allegorical carvings were similar to those at Rosslyn, but, if anything, more flamboyant. When the queen died in 1463, three years after her husband, the construction work was discontinued, but it was still described as being, with the exception of Holyrood Abbey, the 'finest example of decorated English Gothic architecture in the City, with many of the peculiarities of the age'.[1] Following the Reformation, it passed into the possession of the City of Edinburgh. When the North British Railway Company acquired the site in the valley under Calton Hill in the nineteenth century the building was dismantled.

In the fourteenth and fifteenth centuries it was fashionable for wealthy nobles and landowners to endow a church for the maintenance of divine service on a scale of completeness and ceremonial dignity impossible in an ordinary parish church. Over thirty-seven collegiate churches of a size not that dissimilar to Rosslyn were commissioned during the reigns of James II, III and IV and, despite the ravages of the Reformation, survive to this day. Perhaps their benefactors believed that such extravagances would guarantee them a favourable reception in the afterlife. You have also to remember that there was also a lot of one-upmanship going on. In 1429, for example, Sir John Forrester endowed a church at Corstorphine, to the west of Edinburgh; Sir Walter Halyburton followed his lead at Dirleton in 1444, and two years later, Sir David Murray at Tullibardine in Perthshire, and Sir Andrew Gray at Fowlis, did likewise, as did Sir William Creychtoun at Crichton, in 1449.[2]

In the case of William St Clair, we know that his castles were lavishly hung with tapestries and richly furnished, and that he travelled in great state with many attendants. He was therefore a rich and hugely successful man with money to spare; a veritable Scottish Renaissance prince in the making. What do such men do when they reach the pinnacle of their achievement? They build something for which they will be remembered.

In Scotland, the endowment of a cathedral, or at least a chapel, was the next best thing to building yourself a palace, and palaces were not such a good idea as monarchs, especially of that period, tended to become jealous, and, what was worse, acquisitive. No matter how you chose to assert your own self-importance, it needed to be on an impressive scale, and, if not big, then at least exquisite. The more masons and designers you could afford to import from continental Europe in order to achieve this, the better. Moreover, in the case of Prince William St Clair, an appropriate and ideally suitable site was already available, that of the first castle of Rosslyn, abandoned in the previous century. This lay on the high ground to the north-west of his current domicile. Two factors would have contributed towards his decision to use this site. First of all, the foundations, and no doubt remnants of the original structure, would have remained intact. Secondly, some of his Crusader ancestors had already been interred there.

In *Theatrum Scotiae*, published in the seventeenth century, John Slezer, Captain of the Artillery Company and Surveyor of Their Majesties Stores and Magazines in the Kingdom of Scotland, writes that three princes of Orkney and no less than nine barons of Rosslyn were interred in the chapel. What this confirms is that the foundations of the chapel are a great deal older than the chapel itself, and that its vaults do belong to a previous building, and a substantial one at that.

And this, in turn, has led to an intense fascination not only with the interiors of the chapel, but with what lies beneath them; and not just the vaults containing the remains of Rosslyn's previous owners, but whatever else might have been secreted away there over the centuries. On the basis of a claim that the ground plan is a one-third scale replica of the Third Temple, built in Jerusalem by King Herod, it would come as a surprise to discover that the subterranean accommodation was anything other than substantial.

Rosslyn Chapel is 40 feet, 8 inches in height. Its breadth is 34 feet, 8 inches, and its length, 68 feet. There are thirty-two different styles of arch within. The date scheduled for the completion of Prince William's structure is uncertain, given that it was to have been part of a far greater project of cathedral proportions – possibly the choir of a far larger nave – but we do know that when Prince William died in 1484 he was, as was to be expected, buried in the vault, despite the work being incomplete. We also know that an earlier church, approximately 60 feet long, at one time stood in the cemetery lying below, between today's chapel and castle. However, with the knowledge that there was yet another family chapel located within the more modern castle – possibly for use when under siege – it can only be assumed that by then this other chapel would have become redundant.

By this stage, of course, the St Clairs had occupied the site of the present castle for approximately 140 years, adding bits on to it with each generation. It was the 2nd Prince Henry who built the great 50-foot-long dungeon, and created parkland for red and fallow deer. In the next generation, Father Hay explains, for thirty-four years before Prince William turned his attention to building a chapel he was surrounded by great numbers of workmen. They had been kept busy fortifying his castle: shoring up the rock of its foundation, strengthening its walls, and creating a drawbridge.

What emerges, therefore, is a picture of a man of substance who, taking stock of his family's obligations, was determined to protect his interests, be they at Kirkwall on Orkney, his territories in Caithness, or at Rosslyn, to confront the overland approach routes from England. Prince William's titles, observed the historian David Hume of Godscroft, writing in the seventeenth century, 'might weary a Spaniard'.[3] Prince of Orkney, Duke of Olden-burgh, Earl of Caithness and Strathearne, Lord St Clair, Lord Niddesdale, Lord Admiral of the Scots Seas, Lord Chief Justice of Scotland, Lord Warden of the Three Marches, Baron of Rosslyn, Pentland and Pentlands Moor, Baron of Cardain, Baron of Newburgh, Baron of Roxburgh, Knight of the Cockle – the cockle shell being the symbol of pilgrims to the Holy Land – Knight of the Garter, Chevalier of the Ordre de la Toison d'Or, High Chancellor, Chamberlain and Lieutenant of Scotland, there was within the realm of Scotland no loftier being next to the king himself.

Added to which, Prince William's life span itself encompassed the reigns of three Stewart monarchs: James I, James II and James III, all of whom knew they could trust him. His loyalty to the Royal House of Stewart was proven, and he became an indispensable wise old head, to whom they could each, in turn, look for advice. Alas, had he not died four years earlier, he might have been able to successfully mediate in the nobility-led debacle in 1488 which overthrew James III and placed his fifteen-year-old son, James IV, on the throne. While the politics of the age, and the St Clairs' complicated family relationships, have no direct bearing on the actual physical erection of Prince William's chapel, they do help to explain some of the reasons why progress in building it was so slow.

James Stewart, the future James IV of Scotland, was born as the work on Rosslyn Chapel was well under way, and must have witnessed at least some of the construction work at first hand. His second cousin, Lady Margaret Douglas, a granddaughter of King Robert III, was Prince William St Clair's first wife. The first wife of James's uncle, the Duke of Albany, was Prince William's daughter Catherine St Clair, although this was far from being to the St Clairs' advantage since Albany made a career of conspiring against his brother and was eventually exiled for treason. Un-surprisingly, he and Catherine later divorced, but despite the relationship between the Crown and Prince William St Clair being severely tested at times, it remained surprisingly solid. Undoubtedly, this was because all three of the Stewart monarchs, I to III, knew they could rely upon him.

Aged twenty-two, he was charged with the safekeeping of King James I's twelve-year-old daughter, the Princess Margaret, when she was sent off to marry the thirteen-year-old dauphin, later Louis XI of France, in 1436. Such was the impression he made on this occasion that Charles VII of France created him a Knight of the Cockle, a precursor to the French chivalric Order of St Michael. On top of this he was also created a Chevalier of the Ordre de la Toison d'Or, or Golden Fleece, a citation founded six years earlier by Duke Philip III of Burgundy.

There could hardly have been a more stimulating time for a young man to visit France. Five years earlier, Joan of Arc had been burnt at the stake for heresy and sorcery by an ecclesiastical court of the Inquisition, but despite, or perhaps because of, her betrayal by those she had fought for, the English ascendancy over France's northern territories had come to an end. Charles VII, crowned King of France seven years earlier, had grown up under the care of his future mother-in-law, Yolande of Aragon, who, as consort to Louis II of Anjou, laid claim to Sicily, Naples, Jerusalem and Cyprus. The power and reach of the French Court were therefore fabulous: although France was still embroiled in the Hundred Years War with England, Philip of Burgundy, with whom England had previously had an alliance, had recently signed the Treaty of Arras with Charles, returning Paris to the French Crown. The territories which the young Prince William St Clair was in a position to explore stretched as far south as southern Spain. Furthermore, although Princess Margaret Stewart was to die at the tender age of twenty-one, the marriage was immensely astute politically for Scotland, being at the same time a snub to England.

On their journey, St Clair and the princess were accompanied by one hundred gentlemen, twenty clad in cloth of gold with 'chains of gold, and black velvet foot-mantles; twenty in red velvet with chains of gold, and black velvet foot-mantles; twenty in white and black velvet, signifying his [Prince William's] arms which is a ragged cross in a silver field; twenty clothes with gold and blue coloured velvet, which signified the arms of Orkney, which is a ship of gold with a double treasure, and flower de luces going round about it in a blue field; and twenty diversely coloured, signifying the divers arms he had'.[4]

As a bachelor Prince William had no ties or responsibilities, other than to hand over the young Princess Margaret to the French Court. His mission accomplished, he would therefore have had the freedom to explore. He would probably have seen the high Gothic interiors of Notre Dame in Paris, and Chartres Cathedral, rebuilt following a fire two centuries before. He would most likely have taken the opportunity to explore King Charles's southern territories, and with the astonishing ease with which distances were covered on horseback, would almost certainly have wished to visit Teba, in southern Spain, where, in the previous century, his ancestors had so poignantly been killed in battle against the Moors, whose descendants were still dominant in Al-Andalus. The name Al-Andalus was the name given to the territory by its Muslim conquerors, and the Revd Michael Fass, priest in charge of Rosslyn Chapel today, is convinced that this is where Prince William found the inspiration for his future creation, 'echoing that ethereal architecture of the Iberian peninsula which he had seen'.[5]

Prince William and his first wife, Lady Margaret Douglas, were married around 1440, on his return from France aged twenty-six, and began their wedded life in great style. 'In his house he was royally served in gold and silver vessels, in most princely manner, for the Lord Dirleton was his master-household, the Lord Borthwick was his cup bearer, and the Lord Fleming, his carver', Father Hay tells us. He adds that Margaret had serving her '75 gentlewomen, whereof 53 were daughters to noblemen, all clothed in velvets and silks, with their chains of gold, and other pertinents; together with 200 riding gentlemen, who accompanied her in all her journeys. She had carried before her when she went to Edinburgh, if it was dark, 80 lighted torches. Her lodgings were at the foot of the Blackfriars Wynd, so that in a word, none matched her in all the country, save the Queen's Majesty.'

In 1455, James II exchanged the earldom of Caithness for the St Clair earldom of Nithsdale, which Prince William had inherited from his mother. Following the king's marriage to Princess Margaret of Denmark in 1469, William was also obliged to hand over his earldom of Orkney in return for Ravenscraig Castle in Fife. The Orkney Islands, part of Queen Margaret's dowry, were formally annexed to the Scottish Crown by Act of Parliament in 1471. King James was also to receive the Shetland Islands, but these came later. Even without their islands fiefdom however, the St Clairs remained all powerful in Scotland, and it would have been considered strange had the future James IV not attended Prince William's funeral at Rosslyn Chapel, even as an eleven-year-old.

In 1970 a widely acclaimed book, *Falcon: The Autobiography of His Grace James IV, King of Scots*,[6] was published and became an instant bestseller. Its author was the acclaimed playwright AJ Stewart, who astounded historians by filling in the gaps which written testimony to the past had previously overlooked. In her subsequent, autobiographical book, *Died 1513; Born 1929*, which deals with reincarnation, she explains how this was achieved.[7] In recent years she has been living quietly in Edinburgh, but still retains a formidable grasp of the events of 500 years ago, the period in which Rosslyn Chapel was built. On a bright afternoon in the summer of 2005, therefore, I accompanied AJ Stewart on a journey into the past to see if there was anything about Rosslyn or Prince William's funeral that might have somehow lodged in her subconscious. In *Falcon*, her memoir of James IV, her attention to detail is impressive, so much so that her psychic authority of the subject is hard to challenge.

It was a Thursday, and Stuart Beattie, Rosslyn's custodian, had confirmed that there would be no bus tours that afternoon. Even so, when we arrived we found at least thirty visitors milling around. It was a cosmopolitan group: four young Australians consulting their copy of *The Da Vinci Code*, a Japanese husband and wife wielding a digital camera, a Yorkshireman with a divining rod, and some loud, middle-aged Americans who fell reverentially silent in front of the Apprentice Pillar. Nobody paid any attention to us as we explored the choir and the crypt, where AJ said she felt most at home.

Memories of a great funeral and a christening did come to mind. It had been a multicoloured funeral. 'They wore bright colours, but muted them. You didn't want flashing sunlight on jewels. And yes, it wasn't at all unusual to be buried in a suit of armour, especially if you had been on a crusade.' AJ remembered the crypt as something else, perhaps the cellar of an older building, in other words a section of the original vaults. 'That's the one thing about crypts,' she remarked, 'they never change. You don't rebuild cellars if you are rebuilding a house. You start at ground level, and that is why so many Roman foundations have survived. Right back to Thebes. Wherever you go in the world, people make use of the cellars that already exist.'

For AJ there proved to be something hauntingly familiar about the crypt at Rosslyn. 'It doesn't really fit with the building above, does it?' she commented. She was right, it does not. There is something distinctly odd about this chamber. 'I think that there must have been another room, rather similar,' she volunteered after a pause. 'There was another stairway leading to it, rather similar to the one here. But definitely not this one.'

A walled-up cavity caught her attention. There had once been a mediaeval safe and an iron grille, and she stretched out to touch the space above where it had been, as if to feel where the fastenings had originated. 'It was a heavy one', she said. 'Kings had access to knowledge concerning hidden places, often a matter of life or death. That was why a lot of people died so that their secrets didn't get out.'

Returning to the choir, she pointed out the niches high up on the walls, twelve on each side, where she had expected to see figures of the apostles. In the world of pre-Renaissance Catholicism, such figures were considered extremely important. They were brightly painted and made either of plaster or wood. 'If you build a niche you have to have something in it, and if you have an empty niche in a church, the first thing you do is to make a statue.' Such figures would have been among the first items to be destroyed during the Reformation, and since it is on record that Prince William employed numerous carpenters, it seems likely that they would have made carvings that would later have been translated into stone. This was a way of evaluating the scale and design of an image before it was finally approved and put in place.

On the exterior, to the left of the baptistery door, AJ pointed to the lepers' squint, angled on the wall so that those who were unable to enter the church could stand outside and peer through into the interior. 'A most precious thing,' she observed, and crossed herself. 'Leprosy itself came late to Scotland, imported by the Crusades,' she continued. 'Virtually everyone who went on a crusade came home with a skin disease. The lepers' squint was for the unclean people who were kept outside. In mediaeval times almost any skin condition was diagnosed as leprosy. But true leprosy was not as widespread as thought. Lupus, an ulcerous inflammation of the skin, was far more common.' Now there will be those who will dismiss AJ Stewart's observations out of hand, probably on the grounds of her eccentric reputation or that she was stating the obvious, but it is hard to deny that she comes across as being intimately familiar with the mediaeval mind. Because of this, she is a perfect conduit to understanding both the practical and creative thinking behind the chapel's creation.

By his marriage to his first wife, Margaret, daughter of the 4th Earl of Douglas, created Duke of Touraine in France, and a granddaughter of Robert III, Prince William St Clair had a son christened William and, according to Father Hay, four daughters. When Margaret died *c*.1451, he married Marjorie Sutherland of Dunbeath, a great-great-granddaughter of Robert the Bruce, by whom he had a further six sons and seven daughters. Thereafter, according to research completed by the distinguished 21st-century historian Hugh Pesketh, he married for a third time and had further issue, but such records as survive are incomplete.[8]

What is confirmed, as we have already seen towards the end of Chapter 6, however, is that the eldest son, William, having acquired the moniker 'William the Waster', was disinherited: he was passed over for the lands of Herbertshire and baronies of Rosslyn and Pentland in favour of his eldest half-brother, Oliver, and for the earldom of Caithness in favour of William, his second half-brother. Left only with the barony of Newburgh in Aberdeenshire, it comes as no surprise to learn that William the Waster felt hard done by and, following his father's death in 1484, took issue on the subject. To his credit, Oliver appears to have done the decent thing and, ignoring his father's wishes, ceded much of the property back to William, including Ravenscraig, while retaining the Rosslyn estate. An Act of Parliament recognised William as Lord St Clair of Dysart and Chief of the St Clairs, but alas the Waster did not have long to enjoy his reinstatement. He died soon after from a gallstone, the size and shape of a nutmeg.

With the funds at his disposal dramatically depleted, Sir Oliver of Rosslyn, who had by then married a daughter of his Midlothian neighbour, Lord Borthwick, was unable to complete his father's original plan for a full collegiate church, or, as some suggest he intended, a cathedral. Instead, he saw to it that the work on the chapel was finished off. With foresight, the last of the Orkney St Clairs had, prior to his death, endowed his chapel with the income from his lands of Pentland, which further depleted Sir Oliver's financial inheritance. In addition, 100 pounds Scots – approximately £12,000 in today's money – from the will of Oliver's maternal grandfather was bequeathed towards its upkeep, an annual 10 pounds of which was for a priest to sing perpetually for his soul, a practice that was discontinued after the Reformation. The chapel, therefore, now had its own trust fund to draw upon, and thus to some extent relieved the family from some of the financial burden of its running costs.

Alas, the reign of James IV, King of Scots, which had begun so promisingly in 1488, could not have ended more disastrously, either for Scotland or for the St Clairs. James IV, the most brilliant of the Stewart dynasty, had breathed self-confidence into his realm. He was fifteen when he inherited a kingdom which had been destroyed by factional conflict. He began the process of pacifying the Highlands. He introduced learning to the wider population, a practice continued by the followers of John Knox in the following century, and he made his little kingdom a power in Europe.[9] All was well, exceedingly well, and then, alas, he allowed himself, and worse, Scotland, to become embroiled in his bully of a brother-in-law's feud with the King of France, with whom James had signed an alliance. In 1513, hoping to encourage Henry VIII to cease hostilities against Louis XII, James invaded England with an army numbering up to 30,000 men. For Scotland, it was a catastrophe.

It is estimated that 12,000 Scots soldiers died on that terrible day. Twelve earls, fourteen lords, the Archbishop of St Andrews, the Bishop of Caithness and the Bishop of the Isles fell with their king on Branxton Moor at the Battle of Flodden. Having previously incurred the king's displeasure – the reasons are not on record – the 2nd Earl of Caithness, Prince William's second son by his second marriage, was under attainder. When James saw a body of troops arriving to join him, all clad in green, he asked who they were, and, on being told that they were the men of Caithness, decided to pardon the earl. No parchment being available, the king had the instruction inscribed on a drumhead which was cut out and handed to the earl. A rider was rapidly despatched to the Countess of Caithness so that if her husband did not return from the battle, the family inheritance would be secure. It was as well that this was done. The courier was the only member of the Caithness troop to return home. For generations thereafter no St Clair or Sinclair, as the Highland and certain junior branches of the family came to spell their name, would be seen wearing the colour green.

Among the roll call of the Scottish dead that day were 600 Highland Sinclairs; William, 2nd Earl of Caithness; his cousin, Henry, 3rd Lord St Clair, William the Waster's son; and their kinsman, Sir John of Dryden. There were only four men left of the entire Scottish peerage, and their followers had perished in equal proportion. Scotland was left in a state of apprehension and uncertainty.

NINE

✠

The Holy Rude and the Holy Grail

The Rosslyn connection

*I*n an age of atheism and doctrinal retreat, the Holy Rude – or Black Rood, so called because the crucifix in which the splinter of the True Cross was implanted was made of ebony, richly ornamented in gold – remains one of the most priceless symbols of Scotland's Christian sovereignty and, despite the carnage of the Reformation, it defies imagination that it could have been allowed simply to vanish. This was no diminutive object, but stood a substantial 3 feet 9 inches in height. There has to be more to its disappearance than carelessness.

Following King Edward I's invasion in 1296, the mediaeval sovereign reliquaries of Scotland were removed to England by him and were held in London until 1328, when the Treaty of Northampton made provision for the return of the Holy Rude, but curiously not the Stone of Destiny. Could this have been because King Robert knew that the large lump of sandstone held at Westminster was not the genuine article? An unlikely assumption, but worth pondering. Of all of Scotland's State treasures, the Stone of Destiny has grabbed the popular imagination, not least because of its supposed ancestry. It is alleged to be the biblical pillow upon which Jacob, the Hebrew patriarch, rested his head in the Garden of Bethel in Judea, where, at one stage, the Ark of the Covenant was also kept.

The stone is said to have been brought to Scotland via Ireland from Egypt in the sixth century by Fergus Mor Mac Erc, first king of Dalriada, and all subsequent Scottish kings were crowned upon it. On hearing of the approach of King Edward's army, and suspecting his motives, it is said that the Abbot of Scone gave instructions for the genuine stone to be hidden and replaced with a lump of local rock. Both the writer Seton Gordon and the novelist Nigel Tranter are convinced that the genuine stone was hidden in a cave at Dunsinnan in Perthshire and remains there to this day. The 'official' view, however, is that this is based on pure romanticism and there is no evidence to support it.

Eighteen years passed after the Holy Rude was returned to Scotland, then in 1346, Bruce's son, 22-year-old King David Bruce, adhering to the Franco-Scottish Alliance and hoping to distract Edward III from the Siege of Calais, marched into England carrying it at the head of his army. It was a huge mistake. The Scots were soundly defeated at Neville's Cross, near Durham, King David was taken prisoner, and the Holy Rude of Scotland was put on display on a pillar of St Cuthbert's shrine in Durham Cathedral.

Historical accounts are often contradictory. One version of the Holy Rude story insists that this unique artefact was looted with all the other valuables associated with the Church of Rome when that great English cathedral was despoiled in 1540. However, there is another theory which claims that it was retrieved from England seven decades earlier, in 1471, through the diplomacy of Prince William St Clair, when he was sent to London as Scotland's ambassador by James III.[1] This variant certainly presents a far more compelling possibility. And if it is indeed the case then the Holy Rude would certainly have been among the items of value taken from Holyrood Palace to Rosslyn for safekeeping between 1544 and 1548, the period of national emergency known as the 'Rough Wooing', after the Scots had broken off the betrothal of the two-year-old Mary, Queen of Scots, to the five-year-old Prince Edward of England.

To house them we know from Father Hay that a 'treasury' was

built, but its whereabouts remains a mystery. Some zealots insist that it must have been located within the chapel vaults, but why not within the castle? Or was the sanctity of the chapel considered inviolable? Surely not with the Reformation underway? However, these were early days in that particular saga, and by protecting the valuables of Scotland the St Clairs of Rosslyn, as loyal subjects of the House of Stewart, were fulfilling what they saw as their sacred duty. But to just what lengths did that loyalty stretch?

In 1544, Rosslyn Castle came under attack from the English again, for the first time in over two centuries. This time the assault was led by Edward Seymour, the Earl of Hertford, King Henry VIII's commander who later became 1st Duke of Somerset. In the course of his Scottish campaign, his army decimated 243 villages, destroyed 7 monasteries, burned 5 market towns, and razed 4 abbeys, including Dryburgh and Kelso.[2] Rosslyn Castle was severely damaged by fire, but amazingly the chapel was left intact and no mention is made of valuables being seized. In February of the following year, the Scots did win a victory against the invaders at Ancrum Moor, but were severely beaten at the Battle of Pinkie on 'Black Saturday', 10 September 1547.[3]

Only months previous to this defeat at Pinkie, Mary de Guise, Queen Regent of Scotland in the absence of her daughter Mary, Queen of Scots, who had been sent to France for her own safety, wrote an enigmatic letter to Sir William St Clair of Rosslyn, in which she referred pointedly to a 'secret' which she promised not to reveal. In addition, she pledged to 'maintain and defend him be ourself, our pensionaris, servandis, partakers and assistants, that will do for us, in all his actions, causes and quarrels, contraire and against all men that leive, or deny the crown of Scotland and authority thereof', and allocated to him an annual pension of 300 merks.[4] So what was this 'secret' Mary de Guise promised not to betray?

The previous year, a communication had arrived at Rosslyn from the Scottish Lords in Council demanding that Sir William produce, within three days, all jewels, vestments and ornaments of 'the abbay and place of Halyrudhous'. There is no record of Sir William's response, so we are left to speculate as to what these jewels, vestments and ornaments were, where they were being kept, and why it was that Sir William should have been held responsible for them in the first place. Certainly, the contents of Holyrood would have included the Honours of Scotland: the circlet of gold used at King Robert I's inauguration, the Sceptre of Peace, a gift from Pope Alexander VI to James IV in 1494, and the Sword of State, a gift to that same king from Pope Julius II. In times of national emergency it makes sense that these items would have been stored somewhere that was considered safe until the danger had passed, and their hiding place could well have been Rosslyn. But what else might there have been?

In contrast to the Holy Rude, we do know for certain what became of Scotland's other icons. During Oliver Cromwell's invasion of 1651, for example, the Honours of Scotland were taken to the Keith Family stronghold of Dunnottar Castle in Kincardineshire. When Cromwell attacked Dunnottar, they were smuggled out by a servant girl and hidden in a church in Kinneff. They were later transferred to Edinburgh Castle where they were found in 1822 by Sir Walter Scott, who discovered their hiding place from researching old manuscripts.

The whereabouts of Scotland's Holy Rude is central to the mythology surrounding the treasures thought to have been secreted away in Rosslyn Chapel and Castle. Its whereabouts is still a mystery, and one that has increasingly focused on Rosslyn, especially with the publication of *The Da Vinci Code* in 2003. Not only that, the chapel has also come to be associated with the missing wealth of the Templars, if it ever existed in the first place.

In *Theatrum Scotiae*, published in 1693, John Slezer writes that a great treasure, 'amounting to some millions, lies buried in one of the vaults at Rosslyn'. So as to put people off looking for it, he says that it is under the guardianship of a lady of the ancient house of St Clair who, not very faithful in her trust, has long been in a dormant state. Awakened, however, by the sound of a trumpet, which must be heard in one of the lower apartments, she is to make her appearance and to point out the spot where the treasure lies. Whether the vaults to which he refers are those under the chapel or to be found within the castle itself is open to conjecture. Whether the treasure worth millions is in fact the Holy Rude, or one of the many other possibilities which proliferate, is equally unclear. Short of levelling the entire plateau upon which Rosslyn sits, we are unlikely ever to know, and God forbid that we should. An unresolved mystery is far more tantalising than an established truth.

One claim made is that the original stones which formed the foundation for the Ark of the Covenant under the Dome of the Rock in Jerusalem over 2,000 years ago are now to be found within the chapel.[5] A more recent contention, announced by the Edinburgh-based musician Stuart Mitchell and others, is that the 213 cubes set into the roof of the Lady Chapel represent the Devil's Chord, a set of notation proscribed by the Church for inducing altered states of consciousness. The Holy Grail, according to popular belief the vessel used to gather up the blood of Christ at his crucifixion, is thought to have been among the great treasures of the Dome of the Rock, and is said to possess extraordinary powers of healing. An alternative belief is that it was the cup from which Jesus drank at the Last Supper, but not to be confused with the Holy Chalice which contained the wine, and which is among the venerated relics held at the Cathedral of Valencia in Spain. Either way, and whatever it is, many believe it resides at Rosslyn. And, given the outlandish symbolism allocated to so many Christian reliquaries, skulls, bones and body parts, it comes almost as a relief to find such potency associated with a simple goblet, made of clay or stoneware, in preference to human tissue. But then there is the additional 'spiritual' interpretation to contend with.

The passing centuries have served only to blur, excite and exaggerate hypotheses, and mobilise cranks, but there is still a widespread belief that, in mankind's increasingly more desperate attempts to understand the origins of spirituality, at least some of the answers are to be found somewhere in the vicinity of Rosslyn Chapel. This is evident not least in the proliferation of secret societies and cult practices which have sprung up to ruthlessly associate themselves with the Knights Templar and the history of the St Clair Family.

✠

TEN

The Cradle of Freemasonry

Secrets and lies

*W*hat makes people so especially paranoid about secret societies? Is it because there are those amongst us who seriously believe that they are being excluded from something they would like to be part of? Or is it simply fear of the unknown?

In February 2002 members of the reinstated Scottish parliament were asked to reveal their links with Freemasonry. By October, members of the Scottish judiciary were being called upon to set up an independent judicial appointments board to flush out any of their number who might have links with anything considered to be vaguely subversive. To some degree this situation was instigated by Robbie the Pict, a Dunvegan-based political activist undergoing prosecution for recurrent nonpayment of Skye Bridge tolls.

The Scottish law officers who presided over his judicial hearing, Robbie maintained, were all members of the Speculative Society, a shadowy brotherhood entrenched in the Scottish Establishment. The Speculative Society, he alleged, was an unelected, secretive body of men that conspired behind closed doors to undermine the governance of the land.[1] His exposé caused widespread indignation in the media, but came as something of a revelation to members of the society, who, at the time, included the author Alexander McCall Smith, the Scotch whisky writer Charles

Maclean, and the maverick yachtsman Sir Maxwell Macleod, son of the founder of the Iona Community. Up until then, none of them had been aware of the immense influence they wielded.

In the 246 years of its existence, membership of the Speculative Society, an arcane all-male debating club attached to Edinburgh University, has included the writers Sir Walter Scott and Robert Louis Stevenson, but to suggest that it was ever anything more sinister than a postgraduate forum for refugees from Edinburgh's gin-and-bridge set was patently absurd. For those who are interested, a full list of members of the Speculative Society of Edinburgh – 'members who have been admitted to extraordinary privileges, 1947–2000' – is published on www.firstfoot.com/scotchmyth/ssoemembers.htm. However, back in 2002, the claims of the self-styled last Pict in Scotland were taken sufficiently seriously by certain senior opposition members of parliament, who really should have known better, for them to demand a public enquiry. When the accusations proved to be unfounded, and indeed mildly comical, the media and attendant politicians retreated into an embarrassed silence.

It was ever thus. Much of the mystique that so doggedly surrounds Rosslyn Chapel is based on similar hyperbole. Some of it inevitably originates from the St Clair family's unlikely association with the ancient Order of Knights Templar, the clues to this allegedly being found among the carvings of the chapel's interior; the remainder relates to the involvement of certain St Clair family members in Freemasonry, a secretive member organisation that surfaced in Scotland and Ireland during the late seventeenth century and made extensive usage of archaic Templar ritual and symbolism. From such ritual and symbolism springs a widely held theory that the cult of Freemasonry has its origins in the fourteenth century, having been devised as a vehicle to disguise the identity of the persecuted, and finally dispersed, Order of Knights Templar. The fact that such links are impossible to prove one way or the other makes the argument on the one hand all the more intriguing, but, on the other, potentially totally misleading.

So what exactly is Freemasonry? As early as 1599 collectives of artisans existed, providing a loose countrywide support network for one another. Only in the early eighteenth century, however, was the concept of a hierarchical Christian brotherhood of crafts-men spawned, culminating in the creation of a Grand Lodge. The basic underlying principle of Freemasonry today is that it is a worldwide association whose members, from many different vocations, are bound together by shared ideals of both a moral and metaphysical nature; in other words a Christian fellowship. This sounds harmless enough, but three centuries ago, when it first began to evolve into its present form in Scotland, its recruits were predominantly middle and upper class and, following the death of Queen Anne in 1714, supporters of the Jacobite cause, which inevitably gave its members a more clandestine image. Think of all those Jacobite toasts to 'The King over the Water'.

To lend such an organisation the kind of authenticity required for it to be taken seriously, an ancient provenance was required. What more potent symbolism could there be for an exclusive Christian brotherhood to adopt than that of the creators of the Temple of Solomon? And, given that the founders of modern Irish and Scottish Freemasonry were, in many cases, military men[2] – a far cry from the original membership base of humble stonemasons and carpenters that is so often claimed – what better role model could they have found than the ancient defenders of Christen-dom, the vanquished Order of Knights Templar?

Thus was spawned the mythology of Freemasonry, with its attendant secret handshakes, passwords and eccentric rituals. What began as an up-market, clannish social club for aristocrats and skilled individuals, perhaps not dissimilar to the Round Table movement, or the Livery Companies of the City of London, began to be seen, through the quality of its membership, as an all-powerful lobbying elite, with charitable status and international ramifications. Which, of course, was much in the tradition of the

Knights Hospitaller, the Teutonic Knights, and the Knights Templar.

In the early eighteenth century, an age when knightly chivalry was still admired but rapidly making way for modern weaponry, there were those who felt a desperate need to identify with the romance of an altruistic and distant past. In modern terms, masonry, with its associations with trade skills, seems an odd hook upon which to hang the cloak for such an affiliation, but in knightly circles skill was ever of the essence, be it in the production of armoury, strategy in battle, or the creation of a fine piece of architecture. Furthermore, craft agencies flourished throughout Europe and stonemasons were in constant demand. They travelled freely, gaining employment wherever they chose to roam, and hence the term 'free mason' came to be employed. Indeed, in Scotland, no finer example of the skills of free masons is to be found than in the interiors of Rosslyn Chapel.

Here, however, Father Hay, as the official publicist of the St Clairs of Rosslyn, throws in a red herring, maintaining that for centuries the St Clairs of Rosslyn were recognised as hereditary Grand Masters of the Crafts and Guilds and Orders, and, finally, of the Masons of Scotland. Thus, he implies, through the influence of these various guilds, with annual meetings held at Kilwinning, the sanctity of Rosslyn, especially when under attack during the Reformation, was subtly protected.

Hay's evidence relies on two manuscripts, which he describes as charters, but which are, in fact, letters to the 14th and 16th St Clair barons from the Freemen of the Masons and Hammermen of Scotland: the first is dated as around 1601, the second, around 1628. Both letters acknowledge the lords of Rosslyn as patrons and protectors of the deacons, masters and freemen of the masons, the second asserting that 'whereby they [the lords of Rosslyn] had letters of protection and other rights granted by His Majesty's most noble progenitors of worthy memory, whilk with sundrie uthir of the Lairds of Roslin, his wreats, being consumed in ane flame of fire, within the castle of Roslin'. This is an unmistakable reference to the house fire of two centuries earlier,[3] and confirms that Rosslyn's chaplain was not entirely successful in saving the family papers. However, in his 1835 introduction to *Genealogie of the Sainteclaires of Rosslyn,* the historian James Maidment casts doubt on the interpretation from this source that William St Clair was, in fact, the hereditary Grand Master of Scottish Masons, pointing out that 'throughout history there has been an inability to differentiate between stone masons and freemasons, leading to a belief that the two terms are interchangeable'. On the one hand, you have skilled tradesmen; on the other, anyone from a peer of the realm to a travelling salesman. You do not have to be a stone-cutter to become a Freemason.

In his foreword to the 2002 reprint, Robert LD Cooper, Curator of the Grand Lodge of Scotland Museum and Library, endorses this view. 'Maidment considered Hay to be a propagandist', he writes. 'When one turns to Hay for information regarding the hypothesis mentioned earlier in this Introduction there is little or nothing in its support. When one realises that Hay had nothing whatsoever to say about the Knights Templar, Scottish Freemasonry and the Sinclair [St Clair] family's alleged involvement with either of these bodies then it seems that he found nothing either in the family's written history or oral traditions to substantiate such a connection.'

From a Masonic point-of-view, however, Cooper writes that Hay's revelations were significant because they provided a connection between the St Clairs and not Freemasonry but stonemasons. Every mediaeval town had its own local craft guild, the membership of which embraced all of the town's male inhabitants. It goes without saying that Roslin's feudal superior, in the person of the Lord of Rosslyn, would have been Guild Patron. Cooper goes on to argue that 'The subsequent use to which the two letters sent to Sir William by the Masons and Hammermen were put, at the founding of the Grand Lodge of Scotland in 1736, gives an insight into the desires and aspirations of those instrumental in establishing one of the oldest existing Scottish institutions. Whilst their actions are understandable, and many would argue laudable, the consequences for Scottish Masonic history are more problematic given that subsequent writers have failed consistently to understand that those Freemasons in 1736 were intent on creating a suitable pedigree and were not concerned with historical accuracy.' The appointment of Sir William St Clair of Rosslyn, a man of ancient and impressive lineage, as the Lodge's first Grand Master, was a stroke of genius on the part of the innovators.

Freemasonry, already flourishing throughout Ireland, England and mainland Europe, is particularly well documented in Scotland between 1599 and the establishment of the Scottish Grand Lodge of Scotland in the eighteenth century. As early as 1600, the attendance of John Boswell, Laird of Auchinleck, is entered in the minutes of the Lodge in Edinburgh. Many noblemen joined this ancient Order, notably Sir Alexander Strachan, the King's Master of Work. James Neilsone, Master Sklaiter – a fitter of roof slates – to 'His Majestie' was 'entered and passed' in the Lodge of Linlithgow. The minute books of a number of Scottish lodges, which are still in the Register of the Grand Lodge, go back to the seventeenth century and confirm the frequent admission of 'speculatives' as members and officers, especially of the venerable Mother Lodge Kilwinning, of which the Earl of Cassilis was deacon in 1672. Freemasonry thus seems to be a fairly open organisation.

There were three Head Lodges according to the Scottish Code of 1599, of which Edinburgh was 'the first and principall', Kilwinning, 'the secund', and Stirling, 'the third ludge'.[4] The Aberdeen Lodge has records dating from 1670 and notes forty-nine members. The earls of Finlater, Erroll and Dunfermline, Lord Forbes, several ministers and professional men were among them, indicating that prominent members of Scotland's aristocracy were significantly involved. The formation of the Grand Lodge of Scotland, and election of its Grand Master took place on 30 November 1736 at Lodge Canongate-Kilwinning in

Edinburgh. Thirty-three lodges from all over Scotland were represented, and Sir William St Clair of Rosslyn, although not previously enrolled as a Freemason, was invited to become the Grand Lodge's first Grand Master. The association thereafter was to become a family tradition. When Sir William died in 1778, Sir William Forbes, the then grand master paid him the following tribute, the transcript of which is to be found in the archives of the Grand Lodge of Scotland:

> Of this laudable spirit on the part of our worthy Brother, no society can afford a more remarkable instance than our own. Among other marks of royal approbation conferred on his ancestors, for their faithful and valuable services, they enjoyed the dignity of Grand Master Mason, by charters of high antiquity, from the Kings of Scotland. This hereditary honour continued in the family of Roslin under the year 1736; when, with a disinterestedness of which there are a few examples, he made a voluntary resignation of the office into the hands of the Craft in general; by which from being hereditary, it has ever since been elective: and in consequence of such a singular act of generosity it is, that, by your suffrages, I have now the honour to fill this chair. His zeal, however, to promote the welfare of our society, was not confined to this single instance: for he continued almost to the very close of life, on all occasions where his influence, or his example, could prevail, to extend the spirit of Masonry, and to increase the number of the Brethren. It is, therefore, with justice that his name should ever be dear to the Craft, and that we lament the loss of one who did such honour to our institution.

But after this, the St Clair family merged with the Erskines, who inherited the St Clair lands through the marriage of Sir William's only surviving child, his daughter Sarah, and the marriage of her daughter Janet to Sir Henry Erskine, his cousin Katherine St Clair's son. Their son, James St Clair-Erskine, 2nd Earl of Rosslyn, became Acting Grand Master of the Grand Lodge of Scotland from 1810 to 1812, during which time a Grand Masonic fête was held at Rosslyn, attended by over 1,000 masons.

Similarly, the 4th earl served as full Grand Master from 1870 to 1887.

The 5th Earl of Rosslyn was initiated into Lodge 520 Dysart early in 1890, and was passed and raised on the same occasion, a rare privilege. In connection with this, he wrote in his memoirs, 'It is not generally known that the great William St Clair of Roslin, whose memory is always toasted on St Andrew's Day, was with his heirs made hereditary Grand Master of Scotland by James VI, but he with just prudence, asked to be elected by his brethren, an act readily accorded to him.' In his capacity of Junior Grand Warden, the 5th earl, in 1896, laid the foundation stone of the North Bridge of Edinburgh. The following year, on 19 June, he was installed at Rosslyn Chapel as Provincial Grand Master of Fife. For the 5th earl, however, Freemasonry represented 'speeches, song and conviviality', activities which, towards the end of his life, were largely curtailed by his financial collapse. To assume that there was anything more involved, some sinister, self-promoting brotherhood or such like, is extremely self-deluding, especially given his ruin.[5]

Following this, earls of Rosslyn appear to have become distanced from the Grand Lodge of Scotland, with a succession of Scotland's landowning and aristocratic families – Bruce, Baillie, Charteris, Ramsay, Douglas and Orr-Ewing – being elected grand masters in their place. But the ongoing involvement of Scotland's nobility is all part of the camouflage. Clubs, by the very nature of their continuing existence, require to be equivocal to the outsider. When all is said and done, the association between Freemasonry and the Order of the Knights Templar is nothing more than an inspired marketing fiction, the links with the St Clair family of Rosslyn a failure to distinguish between stonemasons and Freemasons, the nature of whom, aside from the degree of elitism they seek to perpetuate, is fairly innocuous.

However, in this regard, much can be and is made of the Masonic degree of Knight Templar, which became popular in the lodges of the British Army during the eighteenth century and hints at some underground network of control. But then again, Freemasonry is a code of practice and loyalty, and RF Gould, author of *Military Lodges*, was of the opinion that the degree of Knight Templar originated from the 'Strict Observance System' that was in practice on the Continent. The Poor Knights of the Temple of Solomon, and their loyalty to one another, regardless of their fate, were seen as suitable role models, but that was all.

Far from being part of a continuing tradition from the start, it was in fact as late as the 18th century that office bearers of Lodge St Stephen in Edinburgh became the first to be initiated as Masonic Knights Templar in Scotland. Choosing a name that reflected an embodiment of commitment and duty was part of the fun. The image undoubtedly suited them, and in 1811 the Royal Grand Enclave of Scotland began issuing charters for the working of the Knight Templar Degree in Scotland. Since then, of course, a veritable forest of unverified fascination has surrounded an association which, the truth be known, simply seeks to harness the nobility of the past for the benefit of the present and the future.

Like it or not, Freemasonry remains a significant social force in Scotland, but there are no bogeymen. Old boy networks operate on all levels of social interaction. Who you know inevitably opens doors, but to suggest that the top jobs are always occupied by, and, when they become vacant, exclusively allocated to Freemasons shows a disturbing lack of self-confidence on the part of those who perpetuate such nonsense. The Grand Priory of Scotland was formalised in 1907, and united with the Grand Encampment of the Temple and Malta in Scotland in 1909. The Grand Lodge of Ancient Free and Accepted Masons in Scotland has its head-quarters in Edinburgh's New Town. The premises are open to the public and the staff work office hours. There is nothing to suggest that it is anything other than a long-established membership organisation dedicated to the betterment of mankind, a purpose which would undoubtedly have won the approval of the founder of Rosslyn Chapel.

✠

ELEVEN

Division of Interests

The Rosslyn inheritance

*I*n mediaeval Scotland, immense personal power was held by those who kept close call with the monarchy. Between the eleventh and sixteenth centuries, the governance of Scotland as exercised by the Royal Court was not so much to be found in Edinburgh or Stirling, but in the Kingdom of Fife, lying on the northern shores of the Firth of Forth. For over 500 years it was the town of Dunfermline, not Edinburgh, that was recognised as Scotland's capital. Among the monarchs who made it their principal residence and who are interred at the great abbey church there are Malcolm III and Queen Margaret, their children Edward, Edgar, Alexander I, Ethelrede, and David I; their great-grandson Malcolm IV; and their great-great-great-grandson Alexander III. The remains of Robert the Bruce, too, his heart having been extracted and despatched on a Crusade, lie beneath the pulpit.

The identifiable associations of the St Clairs with Fife date from 1153, when William the Seemly's grandson, having returned from an ambassadorial mission to Henry II of England, was gifted the lands of Cardain, within the Constabulary of Kinghorn, as a reward. A charter from William the Lion dated around 1170 refers to 'my forest of Carden', which according to Professor Geoffrey Barrow of the History Department of the University of Edinburgh,[1] would have in all likelihood been an area of woodland which monarchs kept for their private hunting; it was the Stewarts' custom to make one of their trusted supporters heredi- tary keeper of such a property.

The name Carden means 'high fortified place' and the site itself, like that of Rosslyn, high up above a ravine, suggests that this may well have been the spot of a much earlier fortification. It is entirely possible that it was on his way here to see his young bride, Yolande de Dreux, that Alexander III fell from his horse and was killed in 1286. However, 'Cardine' is mentioned as being among the possessions of the St Clairs of Rosslyn as late as 1456.

Now, I have a personal interest in this as in the course of my research I came across a reference to Carden in a charter of 1482 connecting ownership of the estate to my own family of Martyne, who later became prominent in St Andrews. Unfortunately, I have been unable to discover when or why it was handed over to them by the St Clairs, if indeed it was from them that it was acquired. The property, it appears, remained in the direct line of the Martyne family until the death of Andrew Martyne without issue in 1549. In 1582, the lands were granted to George Mertyne, who claimed it through his mother, one of the Duries of that Ilk. By this stage, however, the St Clairs were well ensconced in a far more prestigious Fife tenure.

Although Carden was the earliest Fife property acquired by the St Clairs, not a great deal remains today of the once awe-inspiring and all-powerful Ravenscraig Castle, the ruins of which cling to a wind-swept clifftop above a public park to the north of the industrial Fife town of Kirkcaldy. Strategically, with its cannon commanding the mouth of the Forth, it was yet another key installation in the defence of the Scottish realm, and yet another fiefdom which came under the control of the St Clair family.

The Scots had been attacked from the sea in Fife during the Wars of Independence, when Robert the Bruce was in Ireland, and it was left to William St Clair, Bishop of Dunkeld, younger brother of Henry St Clair of Rosslyn, to see them off. Father Hay says, '500 and more of the English fell, apart from the rest who, slipping away in confused flight, when, as they were already embarking on their ships, very many had overloaded their small craft weighed down by too heavy a number, they perished, swallowed up in the waters, or after the enemy band had been killed, who running to their ships in haste, and weighing down the one barge with their weight, sank.' In the following century, as seafaring became more commonplace, the necessity for coastal defences became increasingly more pressing.

From the late fourteenth century onwards a string of North Sea outlook fortresses were purpose-built, from Berwick to Wick. From Eyemouth to North Berwick the waters were closely watched from the battlements of Dunbar, Fast, and Tantallon. Across the Forth, on the north Fife coast was the formidable Bishop's Palace of St Andrews. At Stonehaven, there was Dunnottar; at Cruden Bay, Slains. Serving the St Clair interests of Caithness were the castles of Dunbeath, Girnigo and Sinclair, and Keiss. It was James II who, as part of these coastal defences, instructed the building of a fort at Ravenscraig in the spring of 1460, but not long afterwards he was killed by an exploding cannon at the siege of Roxburgh Castle. It was at the partly constructed Ravenscraig Castle, however, that his widow, Queen Mary of Gueldres, took up residence after his death.

James II's plan had been to build two drum-shaped towers with a gun platform connecting them. The east tower is 43 feet in diameter, and the west, 38 feet, but what is odd is that the west tower is three levels higher than the east, which sat level with the gun platform. Since it was protected by the sea, a low wall enclosed the courtyard behind the towers, and an oblong tower house, possibly a kitchen or storage area, perched at the far south end, but this might have been a later addition. Ravenscraig was James II's pride and joy and, indeed, all the signs were that he intended to keep it for his personal usage. However, his son, having completed the building work after his death, had other objectives in mind.

With his marriage to Princess Margaret of Denmark in 1469,

James III received the Orkney Isles as a dowry settlement. Following the formal acquisition of Orkney to the Scottish Crown two years later, he offered Ravenscraig Castle, its adjoining lands and an annual pension of 40 merks – approximately £30,000 in today's money – to Prince William St Clair in exchange for his Orkney earldom, which he wanted for himself. Prince William accepted; since it was a royal command, he had no option and at least he got something in return. Writing in 1715, his descendant John, Master of St Clair, a fugitive Jacobite on the run, puts a rather different slant on the transaction:

> I had occasion to entertain myself at Kirkwall, with the melancholy prospect of the ruins of an old castle, the seat of the old earls of Orkney, my ancestors; and of a more melancholy reflection, of so great and noble an estate as the Orkney and Shetland Isles being taken from one of them by James the Third, for faultrie, after his brother Alexander, Duke of Albany, had married a daughter of my family, and for protecting and defending the said Alexander against the King, who wished to kill him, as he had done his younger brother, the Earl of Mar; and for which, after the forfaultrie, he gratefully divorced my forfaulted ancestor's sister; though I cannot persuade myself that he had any misalliance against a family in whose veins the blood of Robert Bruce ran as fresh as his own; for their title to the crown was by a daughter of David Bruce, son of Robert; and our alliance was by marrying a grandchild of the same Robert Bruce, and daughter to the sister of the same David, out of the family of Douglas, which at that time did not much sullie the blood, more than my ancestor's having not long before had the honour of marrying a daughter of the King of Denmark's, who was named Florentine, and has left in the town of Kirkwall a noble monument of the grandeur of the times, the finest church ever I saw in Scotland.[2]

Whether young John St Clair's analysis, written as he fled abroad to escape the wrath of King George I two and a half centuries later, rings true or not, his ancestor Prince William and his family were not exactly paupered by the hand-over, which occurred when Prince William was well into his sixties. By the time of his death in 1484, he had already divided his lands and titles among his three eldest sons, but without the Norse earldom of Orkney, now among the titular possessions of the ruling house of Scotland, none of them were eligible to inherit the title of prince. Perhaps this was at the root of Prince William's quarrel with his eldest son, William the Waster?

Despite this, the power base of his descendants in the East Neuk of Fife was to survive for a further 400 years. Travel through Kirkcaldy today and there is a Rosslyn Street, a Loughborough Road, after the family's late-16th-century courtesy title, and a Caithness Street. Indeed, the family held Ravenscraig until 1898, when the gambling debts of the immensely likeable, but financially irresponsible, 5th earl of Rosslyn finally caught up with him. Ravenscraig Castle, Dysart House, and 3,000 acres in Fife were sold to Sir Michael Nairn, founder of the linoleum manufacturing industry which made the town of Kirkcaldy rich during the Victorian era. Time moves on and the popularity of linoleum went into decline when vinyl was introduced during the 1920s. Ravenscraig Castle was taken into State care in 1955, and is today managed by Historic Scotland. Nevertheless, the Fife connection of the St Clair descendants continues.

In 1715, John, the aforementioned Master of St Clair, was attainted for his support of the *de jure* King James VIII, the 'Old Pretender', and for having taken part in the first Jacobite Uprising. He was later pardoned and restored to his lands, but for no apparent reason appears not to have been reinstated in his title of Lord St Clair. Notwithstanding, the ongoing entitlement, although not taken up until recently, duly passed on his death to his younger brother, General James St Clair, who, during the same uprising, had served in Flanders as British Army Quartermaster General. In 1735, General James acquired the lands of Rosslyn from his kinsman, Sir William St Clair who, having no male heir, was last in the direct St Clair male line of Rosslyn.

Genealogy is all too fascinating a game of snakes and ladders.

The St Clair entitlement thereafter was handed on to Henry, another brother, then through four generations of women, starting with their sister Grizel and passing to her daughter, Margaret Patterson of Prestonhall. In 1744, Margaret married John Thomson of Charleton in Fife, and the barony of St Clair line was carried through their daughter, another Grizel, who married Colonel John Anstruther. In 1911 their descendant, Grizel St Clair Anstruther, married Baron Knut Bonde of the Swedish Diplomatic Service, and it is their grandson Baron Knut Harald Jons St Clair Bonde of Charleton in Fife, who is today recognised as heir apparent to the lordship of St Clair.

To add to the confusion, however, in 1782, a barony of Sinclair was reinstated, and is currently held by Matthew Sinclair who descends through the twelfth century Herdmanston line of the family. Meanwhile, in 1766, the lands of Rosslyn were bequeathed to the grandson of General James's younger sister Katherine. Katherine had married Sir John Erskine of Alva. It was Katherine's grandson, Sir James St Clair-Erskine, 2nd Earl of Rosslyn, who in 1805 became heir in entail of Ravenscraig, Dysart and Rosslyn, thus establishing the present 7th Earl of Rosslyn's tenure of the castle and chapel.

All of this family interplay might appear an irrelevant diversion from the mainstream story of Rosslyn Chapel, but not so. Even the more esoteric commentators upon the subject have to acknowledge that for over a thousand years it is the St Clair dynasty which has owned and been responsible for this land and the sites which sit upon it. It is their birthright, and they alone are responsible for guarding the chapel from the speculation over what it might or might not contain.

TWELVE

✠

The Gypsies of Roslin Glen

The postmen of Europe

*A*round the year 1417 there appeared from Germany a travelling group of people who were described at the time as being 'uncouth, black, dirty and barbarous',[1] and who very soon after acquired a reputation for thieving and cheating. The women and children travelled in carts, and they had among them a count and a few well-dressed knights, who carried letters of safe conduct from the Emperor Sigismund of Rome, King of Hungary and Bohemia. To those who challenged them, they explained that they were engaged on a pilgrimage of expiation for some act of apostasy.[2]

Writing 100 years later, the German diplomat and theologian Albert Krantz observed of these same people, in his book *Saxonia*, that they had no country and travelled through the land. 'They live like dogs and have no religion, although they allow themselves to be baptised into the Christian faith. They live without care and gather unto themselves also other vagrants, men and women. Their old women practise fortune-telling, and whilst they are telling men of their future, they pick their pockets.'

Quite how or when the gypsies first appeared to set up a camp in Roslin Glen is not recorded, although attempts are sometimes made to link their Catholic origins with the Knights Templar, which seems unlikely since a gap of 200 years separates them. Another theory is that it was they, and not the Templars, who robbed King Solomon's Temple. Or perhaps they were the fugitive and dissolute descendants of the Templar Knights themselves, under another guise? Similarly, it is not at all clear why they should have come to be so widely known in Scotland, and elsewhere, as 'Egyptians', or 'Pharaoh's People'. This name was supplanted in Scotland later by that of 'tinker', but this naturally derives from the metalwork with which they became so closely associated.

In France they were known as 'Bohemians'; in Germany, 'Tartars' or 'Heydens', meaning 'Heathen', and some of them were said to have originated from India. Byzantine history describes them as soothsayers, magicians and serpent charmers; another source claims that they were the descendants of the outcast Biblical goldsmith Samer, who created the Golden Calf.[3] The Egyptian connection, however, appears to have come from the mouths of the gypsies themselves, who, when asked where they had come from, would reply that it was from a country of their own called Little Egypt. This sounds not dissimilar to the old Scottish legend of the Lost Tribe of Dan, who travelled from Israel across Europe to Portugal and the Basque Country, and ultimately Ireland and Scotland.

The first recorded reference to 'Egyptians' in Scotland appears to be in 1492, in the reign of James IV, but it is more than probable that such people had been appearing on a seasonal basis in May and June for centuries before. More to the point, to begin with, such travelling people were seen as useful since in return for the protection of a great lord, such as Prince William, not to mention the king himself, they could be coerced into acting as messengers and spies. James IV, that most enlightened of Scottish kings, certainly saw the benefits of retaining them. He was fascinated by their knowledge of horses and herbal medicine.

An entry in the accounts book of Scotland's Lord High Treasurer records a payment of 4 shillings to a Peter Ker for attending the king at Hunthall, and receiving letters subscribed to the 'King of Rowmais'. Two days after, a payment of 20 pounds was made at the king's command to the messenger of the 'King of Rowmais'. We do not know the detail, but clearly James made frequent use of their services as postmen and odd-job men. Substantial payments to the 'Egyptianis' are on record, and the king was not averse to recommending their services to others. On 5 July 1506, for example, Anthonius Gawino, described as 'The Earl of Little Egypt', received letters commending him to the king of Denmark, to which country he was about to sail. In this way, the gypsy encampment at Rosslyn Castle rapidly became an intelligence headquarters covering the different countries of mainland Europe.

James V was equally well disposed towards these seasonal visitors at a time when they were being increasingly persecuted throughout mainland Europe. In February 1540, he signed a writ granting protection to 'our lovit Johnnie Faa, Lord and Erle of Littil Egipt'. The same Johnnie Faa was also granted powers to administer justice upon his people 'conforme to the laws of Egypt'. In 1553, this protection of the 'Gypsy King' was renewed during the minority of Mary, Queen of Scots. Amid the Stanks of Rosslyn, on the wooded shores of river or loch, the gypsies and their encampment enjoyed seclusion, plentiful supplies of water and, under the patronage of a great lord, adequate supplies of provisions in return for their 'Tinker' services and the information that they had accumulated on their travels far and wide.

Such was the affection he felt towards them that Sir William St Clair, made Lord Justice General of Scotland in 1559, permitted them to use two towers on his estate, one called 'Robin Hood', the other, 'Little John'. From here they enacted plays based on forty popular ballads surrounding the gallant, but in all probability fictitious, English outlaw Robin Hood. This confirms that these were travelling players, as they would have brought their plays north from England. In mediaeval Scotland, everyone looked forward to the arrival of the Egyptians. That Roslin Glen should have become a summer sanctuary for these wandering folk is entirely appropriate as they headed north with the warmer weather and retreated south with the cold. Roslin Glen was secluded and they were left to their own devices amid the folds of the woodland. You can feel their long-ago presence even now.

For at least four generations, from Prince William to Sir William, and probably before, the St Clairs and the seasonal 'Egyptians' coexisted in harmony, but as Calvinism strengthened its grip on Scotland, the tolerances of a powerful Roman Catholic family became an easy target. In a profoundly orthodox society, the colourful excesses of these travelling people were increasingly being frowned upon and this led, in 1571, to an Act of Stringency that included 'all hangers-on – bards, minstrels and vagabond scholars'. Over the next thirty-three years, following the English and French example, the legal penalties imposed upon gypsies brought to trial increased dramatically. Hanging, drowning and deportation became the norm.

In 1579, an Act of Parliament refers to them as 'the idle peopil calling themselves Egyptians' and recommended that any person found to be a gypsy should be nailed to a tree by the ears, and thereafter have the said ears cut off. The same punishment was soon extended to sorcerers, vagabonds and common thieves. This Act also made it an offence to harbour or give shelter to gypsies and it was not unusual for them to be arrested on sight and hanged from the nearest gallows. Which poses more questions than it gives answers, given that Sir William St Clair was still Lord Chief Justice of Scotland and continued to allow the so-called Egyptians to pitch their camp upon his lands in Roslin Glen. Perhaps he thought it best to turn a blind eye to what was going on in the Protestant judiciary, believing that he, and those under his protection, would get away with it so long as they kept the peace. Only the immediate local community knew of the gypsies' presence, and, like Sir William, harboured no ill against them.

Alas, it was only a matter of time before their cover was revealed and St Clair was commanded to 'pass, search, seek, hunt, follow and pursue the vagabonds' and remove them to the Tolbooth in Edinburgh. He did the best he could. Although an order of execution was issued on several of those taken prisoner, only one was hanged; the remainder were deported. In 1603 the Scottish Privy Council issued an order for the entire race to leave Scotland and never to return, on pain of death. The full severity of Protestant zeal was thus brought to bear upon the people of an outcast race. Thereafter, no mention is made of the 'Egyptians' in Roslin Glen. Not until the late nineteenth and early twentieth centuries were tinkers and travelling people seen once more upon the green.

⊹

THIRTEEN

Rosslyn Chapel Under Siege

The Reformation in Scotland

*T*he end of the sixteenth century saw significant improvements to Rosslyn Castle with the second son of Sir William, Lord Chief Justice, another Sir William, adding the vaults, the great hall and clock tower, and having his architects introduce an impressive 4-foot-wide spiral staircase that led from the basement to the top floor. The aggrandisement was long overdue; it was now well over a hundred years since his great-grandfather Prince William's restoration following the fire.

However, these were uncomfortable times for any family adhering to the Holy Roman faith, and particularly for the hereditary custodians of a celebrated 'house and monument of idolatrie and not ane place appointit for teiching the word and ministratioun of ye sacrementis', as the Presbytery described Rosslyn Chapel in 1589 when they discovered that the minister of Cockpen, the Revd William Knox, a nephew of the great Protestant Reformer John Knox, had participated in a baptism here.[1] Under such circumstances, it is no small irony that the maiden name of John Knox's mother was Sinclair.

A year later, George Ramsay, the minister at nearby Lasswade, was instructed to prevent the burial of Oliver St Clair's widow in Rosslyn Chapel. Adherents to the old faith had been under siege for some time now and this was only the latest attack from the establishment Kirk. Eighteen years earlier, the year before the death of John Knox, the provost and six prebendaries of Rosslyn had resigned in disgust when the chapel's endowments, dating from the time of Prince William St Clair, were removed 'by force and violence into secular hands'.[2] As staunch Catholics, the St Clairs still doggedly refused to succumb to the dictates of the Kirk, but the popular tide was against them.

In 1592 George Ramsay was outraged to find that the chapel's altars remained 'standing haill undermolishit'. When Sir William responded that he would 'defend them as he might', he was accused of being unsound in his religion, and summoned to appear before the Presbytery. The Lord of Rosslyn remained adamant in his defence of what he saw as his private property, but to no avail. In August of that same year he was publicly excommunicated from the pulpit in Dalkeith, the sentence being repeated at Lasswade Parish Church on the following Sunday.

The Catholic Father Hay appears critical but not wholly unsympathetic towards this Lord of Rosslyn, calling him a 'leud man', and inferring that it was his lax morality that encouraged the Kirk to take such a hard line against him. 'He kept a miller's daughter, with whom it is alleged he went to Ireland; yet I think the cause of his retreat was rather occasioned by the Presbyterians, who vexed him sadly because of his religion, being Roman Catholic.'

However, as a wealthy and by all accounts rather arrogant man, it is doubtful that Sir William would have been overdismayed at being excommunicated from the Protestant faith, which he deeply despised. On the other hand, towards the end of 1592, the Kirk was in a position to announce, not without a certain sense of smugness, that the altars at Rosslyn Chapel had been wholly demolished to the satisfaction of the 'Acts of the General, Provincial and Presbyterial Assemblies'. This destruction of Rosslyn's four altars dedicated to St Matthew, the Blessed Virgin, St Andrew and St Peter in the Lady Chapel must have seriously upset him, and might easily have encouraged a retreat to the Emerald Isle.

Thereafter, it seems the chapel was abandoned as a place of worship, its enemies being of the opinion that 'perpetual dripping will wear away the stone'.[3] With no glass, only wooden window shutters, perpetual dripping most certainly did begin to wear away the stone. At the same time, however, there was nothing to prevent Sir William, his sons and his grandsons from being interred in the chapel's watertight, airless vaults, alongside their ancestors. And there was also nothing to prevent the next Sir William, great-great-great-grandson of the chapel's founder, from further embellishing his castle.

Around the year 1610, he married Anna Spottiswoode, daughter of the Bishop of Glasgow, later Bishop of St Andrews, who, in 1635, became Lord Chancellor of Scotland. At the time, the St Clair marriage must have looked like an extremely astute political match from both sides, but events would soon overtake them all. In the meantime, it was this Sir William who built over the vaults, and they are his initials, SWS, which feature, along with the date 1622, above the castle door. The dining room ceiling he introduced featured nine panels decorated with hunting scenes; the central panel contained the arms of St Clair and was also dated 1622.

With his father-in-law's high-profile status as Lord Chancellor, and the rumblings of the Scottish National Covenant movement gaining momentum against the dictates of Charles I, Sir William might be thought wise to have opted out of mainstream public life. Besides, his domestic affairs must have kept him well preoccupied. There was an elder son, also William, who pre-deceased him in France, and seven other sons, one described as 'possessed'. Sundry other natural progeny are also hinted at by Father Hay. Thus Sir William had his hands full.

As the century progressed, Scotland found itself once again spoiling for a fight with the English. But this time it was to be a clash of a very different nature to anything there had been before; a violent confrontation between an English parliament set on deposing its king and determined to undermine Scotland's entrenched loyalties to the royal line of Stewart. An audible gasp was heard throughout the land when Charles I was publicly beheaded at Whitehall on 30 January 1649. At the far end of Roslin Glen, at Hawthornden, the poet Drummond, a devoted Royalist, was reported as being so deeply distressed on hearing the news that it hastened his own end within the year, a demise widely attributed to a broken heart.

At least Drummond was spared the assault upon Roslin Glen, which took place the following year after the Scottish army's ignominious defeat at the Battle of Dunbar, a debacle at which 3,000 Scots were killed and 10,000 wounded. During Oliver Cromwell's march on Edinburgh, first Borthwick Castle was attacked, but it only took a few cannonballs for it to surrender. The siege of Rosslyn Castle was more savage, with Cromwell's commander General George Monck's four pieces of artillery and one mortar gun taking up a position above the river (now the top path) and shelling the north-east and west walls. Sir John St Clair, having just become head of the family – his father having been buried in the chapel on the same day as the Battle of Dunbar – made a valiant stand, but saw his inheritance turned into rubble. Only the most recent part of the castle survived, but even this was pillaged, with the chapel turned over to stabling horses, standard practice with Cromwell's men.

More tragic still was the breaking up of the library. During the last quarter of the sixteenth century, the St Clairs had lovingly accumulated memorials and relics of the Old Faith, rescued from the wholesale destruction of religious houses which had taken place. Of the twenty-one existing manuscripts of the *Scotichronicon* – the first comprehensive history of Scotland, begun in Latin in 1384 by John of Fordoun and continued up to 1449 by Walter Bower, Abbot of Inchcolm – at least five came from the library at Rosslyn Castle. These had remained safe and practically untouched until Monck's soldiers arrived. The unfortunate Sir John was to spend the best part of his life thereafter as a prisoner at Tynemouth Castle, being allowed to return to Rosslyn only shortly before his death in 1690.

Top. The south front of Rosslyn Chapel (from R.W. Billings,
The Baronial and Ecclesiastical Antiquities of Scotland, 1909)

Above. The west front of Rosslyn Chapel prior to the Victorian repairs and
the addition of the baptistery (from R.W. Billings, *The Baronial and Ecclesiastical
Antiquities of Scotland*, 1909)

The eastern aisle (from R.W. Billings, *The Baronial and Ecclesiastical Antiquities of Scotland*, 1909)

The north aisle (from R.W. Billings, *The Baronial and
Ecclesiastical Antiquities of Scotland*, 1909)

Top. Rosslyn Chapel from the east
(copyright © Antonia Reeve)

Above. Rosslyn Chapel from the south
(copyright © Antonia Reeve)

An idealised image of Robert Burns and Alexander Nasmyth
below the arch of the drawbridge of Rosslyn Castle (James Nasmyth.
Reproduced by permission of The Royal Scottish Academy)

The choir. Note the empty plinths. Prior to the Reformation,
these contained statues of the saints (copyright © Dan Welldon)

Looking through from the baptistery towards the choir. The stained glass windows (dating from 1896) above the altar depict the resurrection (copyright © Dan Welldon)

The south aisle. The carving at the top of this picture represents the Seven Virtues
(copyright © Dan Welldon)

The chapel ceiling is divided into five sections featuring daisies, lilies, flowers opening to the sun, roses and stars (copyright © Dan Welldon)

The elegant coil of the Apprentice Pillar. It has been claimed that it shows
the double helix of DNA (copyright © Dan Welldon)

A fierce face of the Green Man, one of more than a hundred versions
based on the same theme (copyright © Dan Welldon)

The top half of the Mason's Pillar. Pre-Victorian images of this column show the centrepiece as undecorated (copyright © Roddy Martine)

Top. The central carving on the Mason's Pillar depicts an angel playing bagpipes
(copyright © Roddy Martine)

Above. On the footpath through Roslin Glen, high above the River North Esk,
is an outcrop of rock known as the 'Lover's Leap'. Carved into the lower portion
is a face; some say that it is that of a monkey; others say that it is a fish
(copyright © Roddy Martine)

The remains of the 16th-century Hospitallers of St John chapel at Balantrodoch, below the village of Temple, ten miles from Roslin village. It sits on the foundations of the one-time Preceptory of the Knights Templar, and some of the stones from the original building were used in the construction of the north wall (copyright © Roddy Martine)

The entrance to Wallace's Cave in the cliffs of Gorton, seen through trees from the opposite river bank of the North Esk (copyright © Roddy Martine)

Top. Rosslyn Castle rises spectacularly above the river gorge of Roslin Glen.
In the background, the Pentland Hills (copyright © Roddy Martine)

Above. Rossyln Castle from the glen, c. 1830 (Revd John Thomson of Duddingston.
Reproduced by permission of the Hunterian Art Gallery, University of Glasgow)

In his absence the castle was part sold and part mortgaged to cover his debts, but recovered at some later stage by his younger brother James, who through his second marriage to the widow of Captain George Hay became Father Richard Hay's stepfather. This Sir James St Clair, by all accounts a good and worthy man, did his best to repair the damage to the estate, but concentrated his efforts largely on improving the grounds rather than the interiors. He planted woodland and a garden, improved the parapets of the bridge over the River North Esk, and introduced a gate despite the funds at his disposal being limited. Although they were not exactly impoverished, the once fabulous wealth of the St Clairs was significantly reduced.

On 11 December 1688, shortly after the Protestant William of Orange landed in England to displace the Catholic James VII and II, a mob from Edinburgh and some of the Roslin villagers took it upon themselves to storm the castle and destroy anything that they considered to be even vaguely popish or idolatrous. It was a sad state of affairs, and thereafter the castle, and its policies, fell rapidly into almost irreparable dilapidation. Father Hay was present on that sorry night and writes of the chapel being 'defaced by the rabble . . . after the castle had been spoiled, where I lost several books of note, and amongst others, the original manuscript of Adam Abel, which I had of my Lord Tarbat, then Register.'

By his first marriage, Sir James had two sons, the eldest being another James, who was killed in Ireland in 1690 at the Battle of the Boyne. That left only his younger son, Alexander, who was succeeded in turn by his eldest son William, last of the 700-year-old direct male line of St Clair of Rosslyn. All families have their personal tragedies, and although this William fathered three sons and five daughters by his wife Cordelia, daughter of Sir George Wishart of Clifton Hall, all but his daughter Sarah predeceased him. Death so often came at an early age to families in those days, and that was why it was considered so important to marry young and to have at least a round dozen children. Such correspondence as survives for the historical record, even into the nineteenth century, in almost every case makes enquiry after the health of the recipient, especially when the survival of a dynasty was at stake. After all, the dynasty and the continued possession of land through the male line were considered to be all that really mattered. The continuation of the family name was of paramount importance. And no doubt this is why, in 1735, Sir William, 19th Baron, made over the Rosslyn estate to his kinsman, Colonel, later General, Sir James St Clair, a respected diplomat and member of parliament.

The general had no sons to inherit, but he did have brothers, and Sir William probably felt that he had no choice but to keep faith with the St Clair name. Although domiciled at Dysart House, the elegant mansion which he had instructed the Fife-based Adam family of architects to build for him, General James spent much of his life overseas. That did not prevent him, however, from showing a great interest in his inheritance. At some stage he must have been advised that there was little hope of the chapel at Rosslyn surviving into the future at all were not something done to make it wind and watertight. It was therefore authorised that the windows be glazed, the floor relaid and the controversial boundary wall be built, shielding the chapel from the glen below. In the manner of the age, Rosslyn Chapel was thereafter regarded as little more than an elaborate countryside folly.

The general had five brothers, the eldest having been the Master of St Clair who was attainted, and later pardoned, for his support of the 1715 Jacobite Uprising. There were also five sisters, and after the general's death, his properties went first to his brother Henry, who died without issue, then, since their other brothers had predeceased them without progeny, to Grizel, their eldest sister, who had married John Patterson of Prestonhall. The Fife and Rosslyn estates then passed to their son, Colonel James Patterson, who died unmarried.

Colonel Patterson had a sister, Margaret, who was the direct ancestor of Baron St Clair Bonde, but after her brother James's death, the Rosslyn inheritance passed to her Aunt Katherine, her mother's younger sister. Katherine was married to Sir John Erskine of Alva, and with the succession in 1805 of their grandson, James Erskine, son of Janet Wedderburn, granddaughter of the last St Clair of Rosslyn in the direct male line, it was the beginning of an entirely new Rosslyn dynasty. A dynasty whose representatives would, one suspects, have been both amazed and deeply appalled had they even the slightest inkling of the blasphemous sensationalism which two centuries later would begin to envelope their family chapel.

✠

FOURTEEN

Rosslyn and the Bloodline of Jesus

Mediterranean sunshine

One of the more eccentric claims of recent hagiography is that Her Majesty Queen Elizabeth II of the United Kingdom of Great Britain and Northern Ireland and of Her Other Territories, Queen, Head of the Commonwealth, Defender of the Faith, is descended from the great-great-grandfather of the Prophet Mohammed. This startling claim stems from the marriage in 1372 of her ancestor Edmund of Langley, fifth son of Edward III of England, to Isabella, daughter of Pedro the Cruel, who was descended from the Caliphs of Cordoba, and therefore from the senior branch of the Qoreish ruling dynasty of Mecca through the Prophet's great-granduncle, Abd Shams, the banker.[1] Edmund of Langley's great-grandson became Edward IV. His great-granddaughter was Mary, Queen of Scots, with whom Her Majesty is connected through cousin marriages over twenty-two times.

An equally intriguing, and entirely sacrilegious, claim is made that, in a similar way, the bloodline of Jesus, his having fathered children by Mary Magdalene, has passed into the Merovingian–Frankish dynasties of France and also into Scotland's Royal House of Stewart. None of this sounds so entirely daft in the light of the regular assertion of that eminent Scottish genealogist, the late Sir Iain Moncreiffe of that Ilk, who maintained that literally everyone in Europe, be they lord or peasant, was descended from the eighth-century emperor, Charlemagne.[2] It was Sir Iain's conviction that all ancestors are interesting, for they are all necessary in handing down life to us even if they lived long, long ago. Had Charlemagne not come of such vigorous stock, and had his third queen, Hildegard, never been born, there would have been no George Washington or George III, no Herman Goering or Winston Churchill, no President Chirac, no Tony Blair or George W Bush.

Depending upon your faith, there is something deeply shocking, and, at the same time, compellingly grotesque, about rewriting received history, especially when it is arguably the greatest story ever told. It may be salutary to recall that it was on a considerably lesser charge that Thomas Aikenhead, a young divinity student in Edinburgh, was found guilty of blasphemy and hanged on the gallows of Leith Walk. And that was only just over three hundred years ago.[3]

Conceivably Jesus of Nazareth did marry Mary Magdalene, as both *The Holy Blood and The Holy Grail* and *The Da Vinci Code* assert. In his position as a rabbi there would have been nothing untoward about this. Under the terms of Jewish Mishnaic Law it would have been expected. However, such a union has to be totally unacceptable for Orthodox Christians, for whom the words of the Bible are inalienable. Attention is directed in both books towards a gospel of Mary Magdalene, a Gnostic manuscript excised from the Holy Bible during the fourth century.[4] Why did this occur? The explanation given for this action is that in this Gnostic text Mary is seen to have been granted precedence over the other disciples. From there, it is easy to imagine how steps might have been taken by certain misogynist members of the Holy Roman Church to suppress the contents and blacken her name, casting her instead as a prostitute. Such speculation becomes truth in the fanciful claims inherent in both *The Holy Blood and The Holy Grail* and *The Da Vinci Code*.

The storyline then progresses to Marseilles, where Mary, the wife of Jesus of Nazareth, and their family, under the protection of

Jesus's disciple, or possibly uncle, Joseph of Arimathea, whom mediaeval tradition portrays as the custodian of the Holy Grail, are said to have fled following the Crucifixion. Tradition has it that they arrived in a boat with no oars after narrowly escaping death during a storm at sea. With them on the boat was a young girl known as 'Sarah the Egyptian', who is commemorated by a statue in the town of Les Saintes-Maries-de-la-Mer. There are caves in which it is claimed the fugitives took refuge, and a celebration and gypsy festival is held here each year on 24 May, Sarah's feast day. Could there be a possible connection between this Sarah and the gypsies of Roslin Glen? I would not want to dismiss the idea out of hand.

A further elaboration on the Magdalene story is pursued in various writings, which reveal that there is a strong possibility that this Sarah, and indeed Mary herself, was a black African, which is not at all improbable, given the geographical location of the Holy Land, and would explain the widespread cult of the Black Madonna which emerged throughout southern France in the first millennium.

Tradition indicates that Mary died around AD 42 in either Aix-en-Provence or Saint-Baume. The latter is today revered as a holy mountain situated between the towns of Var and Bouches-du-Rhône, and has become the centre of Provençal Christian mythology. The high walls around the villages were constructed in the fifteenth century to protect them by King René, prince of the House of Anjou, and Mary's remains are said to be conserved in the crypt of St Maximin.

Far more critical to the agenda of the current promulgators of discord, however, is the meaning of the word *sangraal*, which was employed by early chroniclers to describe the entity of the Holy Grail which tradition maintains Mary had in her possession. Everything boils down to inventive modern interpretation. When the word is broken after the 'n' to form 'san graal' it means 'holy grail' or 'holy cup', but when broken after the 'g' it becomes 'sang raal', which in Old French can only be interpreted as meaning 'blood royal'. Attention is then drawn to the Bible, and Revelation 12: 1–17 where St John the Divine refers to a woman 'clothed with the sun, and the moon under her feet, and upon her head a crown of twelve stars', and the persecution of her seed. 'And the dragon (that old serpent, called the Devil and Satan which deceiveth the whole world) was wroth with the woman, and went to make war with the remnant of her seed, which keep the commandments of God, and have the testimony of Jesus Christ.'

Two strands of opinion have thus evolved. The first interprets the grail as a physical object, ie: a drinking vessel or cup. The second asserts that it takes the form of a woman, the view taken in *The Da Vinci Code*. A millennium after the crucifixion of Jesus, knightly Europe became obsessed with the former, which was embedded in the grail legends of Celtic invention: Chrétien de Troyes' *Story of the Holy Grail* written in the twelfth century; Wolfram von Eschenbach's poem *Parzival* dating from the thirteenth century; the Arthurian sagas of the fifteenth century, culminating towards the end of the nineteenth century with Sir James Frazer's *The Golden Bough*, and Richard Wagner's epic opera *Parsifal.*

To create a plausible historical perspective, however abortive, others have doggedly set out to establish that the 'sang raal', otherwise the bloodline of Jesus Christ and Mary Magdalene, has passed through progressive royal marriages within the Merovingian–Frankish and Carolingian dynasties of Europe to the present day. On that basis, by subscribing to Sir Iain Moncreiffe's received wisdom, it could be said that we are all of us descendants of the Son of God, which is what the Church has been telling us all along.

Laurence Gardner, in his books *Lost Secrets of the Sacred Ark* and *The Magdalene Legacy*, takes it a step further towards mediaeval Scotland, or rather backwards by a thousand years, by connecting the bloodline of Jeremiah to the first-millennium Celtic kings of Ireland and Scotland, which explains how, in the sixth century, Scotland became home to the Old Testament Stone of Destiny. For serious academics, this is all complete and utter hokum, but has certainly not deterred many from pursuing this line of enquiry.

In *The Forgotten Monarchy of Scotland*, the self-styled Prince Michael of Albany, claimant to the Scottish throne, and a most engaging character as I have discovered, asserts that from the union of Tamar Tephi, daughter of King Zedekiah of Judah, and Eochaid, High King of Ireland, in around 586 BC, were descended most of the royal lines of Ireland, not least the Dal Riata – the Royal House of Dalriada, through which all kings of Scots were able to trace their ancestry from the biblical kings of Judah, from the princes of Greater Scythia, and from the pharaohs of ancient Egypt. Writing a review of *The Forgotten Monarchy of Scotland* at the time of its publication in 1998, I felt compelled to ask why it was that Michael sought only after the throne of Scotland when there was so obviously a far larger one on offer?

The key to the puzzle of Mary Magdalene's status and that of her descendants, however, as outlined in *The Da Vinci Code*, is that great Renaissance genius Leonardo da Vinci's masterpiece *The Last Supper* created for the refectory of the Convent of Santa Maria delle Grazie in Milan. This extraordinarily powerful image was completed in 1498, around the time that the building of Rosslyn Chapel was discontinued, but its fascination for the conspiracy theorists lies with the figure seated at the right hand of Jesus, and reclining away from him – an unbearded and distinctly feminine face hitherto assigned to St Peter, but which, in the light of contemporary revelation, must surely be that of Mary Magdalene. I find this conclusion perfectly plausible, but it is strange that it has never been considered before.

No doubt Dan Brown would be astonished to find a Victorian tapestry featuring this very image hanging in the dining room at Rosslyn Castle. Why had this particular artwork been chosen to hang in the castle, and by which member of the St Clair family and when? No one can be sure, but there it is for all to see. Pure coincidence? The believers shake their heads knowingly.

In a monumental parody of all of this, *The Da Vinci Code* tracks down the living survivors of the 'sang raal' to a cottage beside Rosslyn Chapel, hotly pursued by sinister factions within the Church of Rome and protected by a bewildering web of arcane intrigue ranging from the Cathars and Knights Templar to the Rosicrucians, an esoteric grouping which claims a provenance in the glory days of Ancient Egypt. At all times lurking in the background is the shadowy Prieuré de Sion. Is it any wonder that the tour operators have been beating a path to the chapel gates?

⊹

FIFTEEN

Idolatry of the Head

What became of the head-shrine of Queen Margaret?

*A*t the height of the purge of the Knights Templar in France it emerged that it was a common practice among monks of the Order to worship a reliquary in the shape of a head. Known as 'Baphomet', the interior of this sacred shrine was said to contain head bones that, when invoked, induced fertility, a curious boast given that the Order was betrothed to celibacy. Variously described in the prosecution transcripts, this object was never found. However, Tim Wallace-Murphy in *The Templar Legacy and the Masonic Inheritance Within Rosslyn Chapel* links Baphomet with the severed head of John the Baptist. Hugh Schonfield in *The Essene Odyssey* infers that Baphomet was a woman symbolising wisdom. Laurence Gardner in *The Magdalene Legacy* goes so far as to suggest that the head was not that of a man at all, but of Mary Magdalene. Notwithstanding, one of the accusations levelled against the Knights Templar was that they were followers of the idolatry of the head.

Yet why such a fuss should have been made about this is baffling since throughout the Christian world head-shrine worship was commonplace. In June 1566, the skull of Queen Margaret, now St Margaret, enclosed in its own reliquary, was brought to Edinburgh Castle from the Lady Chapel in Dunfermline Abbey at the request of Mary, Queen of Scots, who was expecting her child, the future James VI. St Margaret's head-shrine, she had been told, was also associated with fertility. Two years later, when Queen Mary fled to England, the head-shrine was returned to the monks of Dunfermline, who by then had taken up residence at Craigluscar, a house in Fife that was owned by the Durie family, long-term retainers of the abbey. However, as the Presbyterian faith was rapidly gaining momentum, it was thought unsafe for such a valuable Catholic reliquary to be retained in Scotland. In 1597, it was therefore entrusted to John Robie, a young apprentice on his way to study at the Scots College at Douai, north of Paris, where it was venerated over the following two centuries.

So what did it look like, this head-shrine of St Margaret? Father Hay, who writes that he saw it in 1696, possibly at Douai – although it is equally possible that by then it was back in Scotland – describes it as a bust of silver 'whereupon there is a crown of Silver gilt, enriched with pearls and Precious Stones. In the Pedestal, which is of Ebony indented with silver, her hair is kept and exposed to the view of everyone through a Glass Crystal. The Bust is reputed the third Statue in Doway for its valour [value]. There are likewise several Stone, Red and Green on her Breast, Shoulders and elsewhere. I cannot tell if they be upright, their bigness makes me fancy that they may be counterfitted.'

In terms of destruction, the Reformation has a great deal to answer for: throughout the land, many priceless Church treasures were either destroyed, hidden from sight or sent abroad for safekeeping. For protection, the remainder of St Margaret's relics in Scotland, together with those of her husband King Malcolm, were taken to Flanders and eventually found their way into the possession of Philip II of Spain, who placed them in the Royal Monastery of the Escorial in two caskets entitled 'St Margaret, Queen and St Malcolm, King'. It was from this source that Bishop Gillis of the Eastern District of Scotland obtained, in 1863, the relic of St Margaret that is today a treasured possession of St Margaret's Convent in Edinburgh.

St Margaret's Convent is an Edwardian villa in close proximity to the original seminary, established in 1834 as the first post-Reformation religious retreat of its kind in Scotland. It was here that I was shown two reliquaries of St Margaret by the appropriately named Sister Margaret. The larger of the two, that acquired by Bishop Gillis from Spain, is housed in an ornate bronze and gold basilica designed by the Anglo-French architect Augustus Pugin at some stage before his death in 1852. At the centre, contained within a glass vial, is a piece of the saint's shoulder blade. It is claimed that the second, much smaller, reliquary contains tiny bones belonging to St Andrew and St Margaret, and the small case attached to the back displays a lock of hair allegedly cut from the scalp of John the Baptist. Unbelievers might find all of this a trifle bizarre in our modern world, but the veneration of saintly body parts has always been an integral part of the Holy Roman faith, admittedly a facet of that religion upon which, during the Reformation, its detractors declared open season.

'Its amazing what turns up,' said Sister Margaret, a kindly lady who welcomed me without asking why I was so interested. 'For years we made use of some silver plates in Communion. Then we discovered that they had originated from Holyrood Abbey in the reign of David I.' These are now on display at the Royal Museum of Scotland in Edinburgh. There is no record, alas, as to what became of St Margaret's bejewelled head-shrine. It simply disappeared from Douai and the most common explanation is that it was probably stolen or dismantled in 1789, in the early days of the French Revolution.[1]

A twentieth-century copy, which features artificial stones, is currently on display in the refurbished Abbot House in Maygate, Dunfermline, open to visitors throughout the year, but the myths surrounding it are manifold. Since Father Richard Hay is the last person we know to have seen the original, both as a novice and later when Canon Regular at Sainte-Geneviève's in Paris, there is an outside possibility that he might just possibly have brought it back to Scotland with him when he returned to Edinburgh in

1719. Hay was present when the Protestant mob attacked Rosslyn Chapel and Castle in 1688. In his account of this, he seems more preoccupied with the destruction of the library, than what took place in the chapel. He was certainly aware of the vaults, and as chaplain to his stepfather, would, although not himself a St Clair, have been privy to family secrets. Knowing that the vaults remained undefiled, he possibly considered it best not to draw attention to them, or anything which they might feasibly have contained.

By the early eighteenth century, after one hundred years, it might have been thought safe to return the head-shrine to Scotland, especially if it was in Father Hay's keeping and he was taking it to Rosslyn Chapel. Remember that during the short period before James VII and II was exiled from the British throne in 1690 by his daughter Mary and son-in-law William of Orange, Roman Catholics in Britain enjoyed a brief respite from persecution. James's second marriage to the Catholic Mary of Modena, and the birth of a son and heir in 1688, the future *de jure* King James VIII, caused widespread optimism among British Catholics, not least in Scotland. Since, at this stage, Rosslyn Chapel was a neglected ruin, where better to conceal something truly precious until it could be revealed in all its splendour? And especially if there were other artefacts already hidden there. As the family historian, Father Hay would have known exactly what was there and where it was stored, but he is unlikely to have put it in writing.

Wealthy mediaeval families such as the St Clairs, their roots deeply entrenched in the nation state which their ancestors created, saw themselves, not without justification, as hereditary guardians of the past. Such sentiments may have become dissipated with the religious and political upheavals of the second millennium, but what is a millennium but a blip in time? Everything, as has been proved again and again, is cyclical. The oracles of the past knew this better than anyone. In spiritual terms the past, the present, and the future are as one.

As late as 1995, Keith Laidler, author of *The Head of God: The Lost Treasure of the Templars,* had come to Scotland to search for the Stone of Destiny when he sidetracked to visit Rosslyn Chapel. Having already concluded that the Holy Grail was nothing less than the embalmed head of Jesus, it did not take him long to decide that this was undoubtedly a place where something precious was hidden and, stepping inside, his eyes were drawn to the carving of a crucifix which, instead of showing the full body of Christ, features only his head. He also asserts that the carving of the Master, high up on the ceiling, has been tampered with to remove its beard, and that it is yet another interpretation of 'the head'. This, he wrote, was the proof he had been looking for and from then on became convinced that the skull of Jesus, in all probability the same 'Baphomet' that was venerated by the Knights Templar, lies immediately below the Apprentice or Prince's Pillar. For a brief diversion it was also suggested that the skull was actually concealed within the column. However, subsequent tests proved the stone to be solid.

Such theories are obviously anathema to the Catholic Church posing, as they undoubtedly do, a direct attack upon its teachings on the Resurrection. To add insult to injury, around such profanity has emerged the invention of the Priory of Sion, or Prieuré de Notre Dame de Sion, which has to be one of the most successful surrealist hoaxes of the twentieth century. Church authorities must sometimes regret the passing of a time when such heresy and its exponents were rather more easily disposed off.

✠

SIXTEEN

Father Bérenger Saunière and the Prieuré de Sion

Rosslyn in the Languedoc

*I*n southern France, at some stage during the twelfth century, evolved the Cathars, a Gnostic religious sect who set themselves up in the *départements* of the Aude and the Ariège. The word *cathari* in Greek means 'purity'. Central to the Cathar faith was duality – the battle between good and evil on earth – a form of primitive Christianity which would inevitably bring it into conflict with the Roman Church. If God is all-powerful why do terrible things occur in the world? Orthodox Christianity accepts that in this manner is mankind, and its faith, tested. Dualism insists that good and evil are primary energies in opposition to each other, and that in the shifting balance between them, evil, more often than not, triumphs. From this viewpoint arises the concept of Satan having created the world.

The home base of the Cathars was the castle of Montségur, perched high on a ledge dramatically overlooking the surrounding landscape. When, in 1208, Pope Innocent III launched against them the only Crusade ever conducted on European soil, they were forcibly extracted from their formidable fortress and individually incinerated. However, the night before Montségur surrendered, so the story goes, four of the monks slipped away under cover of darkness with a great treasure. This treasure is believed by many to have been the Holy Grail, in whatever shape or form it then existed. The parallels with Rosslyn are already apparent.

Skip forward six centuries to 1885 and an impoverished cleric called Bérenger Saunière becomes priest to the 200 souls of Rennes-le-Château, south of Carcassonne in the Languedoc region, close to the French Pyrenees. Saunière's career began on a poor stipend, yet a year later he came into a great fortune, reputed to have been a bribe from the Vatican in return for his silence. While renovating his church, it is said, he had come across a hidden parchment and codex hidden within a stone pillar. This document, it is alleged, connected Rennes-le-Château with the Holy Grail, the Ark of Noah, the Ark of the Covenant, the treasures of the Temple of Solomon, and, ultimately, Rosslyn.

For the past six years I have been in the habit of visiting friends who have a house on the Costa Brava coast of Catalonia, less than an hour's drive from Perpignan on the French–Spanish Border, from which it takes a further two hours to reach Rennes-le-Château. On a visit to Perpignan in 1963, the Spanish painter Salvador Dali, born relatively nearby at Figueres, described the railway station there as the centre of the universe. Dali may have been onto something. As a surrealist, he was probably in on the joke too, and on my 2005 trip to the region, despite my reluctance to indulge myself in yet another flight of fancy relating to *The Da Vinci Code*, the urge to investigate the Bérenger Saunière connection with Rosslyn became irresistible.

'Every eight years, the planet Venus forms a pentagram over Rennes-le-Château,' I was told by a knowledgeable friend who accompanied me. 'A pentagram is the geometric shape featured in the ancient rites of resurrection. Venus is Mary Magdalene's star. It's also the Morning Star, the star of Jesus.' I attempted to nod in a suitably enthusiastic manner, not having a clue what she was talking about. 'Are you also aware that the Roseline, "Le Serpent

Rouge", the North–South meridian that bisects Rennes-le-Château, if it is extended, also passes directly through Rosslyn Chapel?' Again, I was lost for words. I had come to southern France to find out what I could about the Cathars. I had no idea that I would be entering into some vast interconnecting cosmic ground plan. 'Did you remember to bring your sunglasses?' I responded meekly.

The warmth of the Mediterranean sunshine was getting to me and I was beginning to enjoy myself. The pottier the invention, the more irresistible it becomes. And it is hard to find anything pottier than either the saga of Bérenger Saunière or the sublime surrealist invention of the Prieuré de Sion. Added to this, the scenery of the Languedoc, the region in which both Rennes-le-Château and Montségur are located, loosely described as the foothills of the Pyrenees, was rather more spectacular and seductive than I could ever have imagined. There is something inexplicably challenging about this landscape of remote villages and mountain fortresses. You can almost smell the conspiracy. Others too have felt this way.

Prompted by the young German historian Otto Rahn,[1] who mysteriously died while off duty at Dachau Concentration Camp in 1938, Heinrich Himmler's Nazi archaeologists, the Ahnenerbe-SS, searched the district for the vanished Cathar/Templar treasure during the Second World War, but none was found. What emerged instead, however, was the inspiration for Steven Spielberg's film *Raiders of the Lost Ark*. In *The Holy Blood and The Holy Grail*, it is the authors' contention that the treasure of Montségur, which in their analysis consists of scrolls outlining the genealogy of Jesus's surviving family, was taken for safekeeping to the remote nearby village of Rennes-le-Château. In the late nineteenth century, the story continues, they were unearthed by Father Bérenger Saunière, who proceeded to blackmail the Vatican and, as a result, became fabulously rich.

Saunière was either an enigma, or a masterly practical joker. No one has so far been able to reveal where his sudden good fortune actually came from, only that he was suddenly rich enough to build houses and roads. Yet when he died he was penniless. Clandestine intrigues proliferate. Accused of illegally selling Masses, he was exonerated by the Vatican, but nevertheless it is hard not to believe that something unscrupulous must have been going on. In reality, the money could easily have come from his wealthy mistress, Marie Denarnaud, who lived until 1946; this would explain why, despite appearing weathly during life, Saunière died insolvent. However, Marie too was considered a bit weird and was once reported as having been seen burning franc notes in the garden. Just as well the Euro had not been invented.

One of the more bizarre theories attached to the Saunière saga surrounds his purchase of a copy of the seventeenth-century French artist Nicolas Poussin's *Les Bergers d'Arcadie*, the original of which hangs in the Louvre Museum in Paris. It shows three half-naked shepherds and a rather brazen shepherdess gathered around a tomb upon which is the inscription 'ET IN ARCADIA EGO', which translates as 'I am also in Arcadia [paradise]'. In the background is a hilltop that closely resembles that of Rennes-le-Château. Nobody has suggested that Saunière, a local boy, might just have liked the view. What subsequently fuelled the speculation is that there is a similar tomb at Argues, only a few miles distance from Rennes-le-Château, which, when opened in the 1950s, was found to be empty.

Cathars, Templars, mystic messages from long ago. No wonder there are those who draw parallels with Rosslyn. Certainly the dusty little French hilltop town of Rennes-le-Château, with its terracotta roofs, is an equally atmospheric place. St Maria Magdalena, Saunière's ornamented church; the Villa Bethania in which he lived; and La Tour Magdala, the small cliff-top tower he built in order to house his library, are certainly unusual. Over the porch lintel of the church is the inscription 'Terribilis est locus iste', meaning 'This place is terrifying'. Once again, was this a reference to the village, to the inhabitants, or to the remoteness of the surrounding landscape? Did Father Saunière, who was after all a man of God, see himself as an outcast? Or was he simply a convert to surrealism and having a joke at everyone else's expense?

I was not at all sure what I expected to find inside St Maria Magdalena. An early twentieth-century parody of Rosslyn Chapel, perhaps? Although on a significantly less ambitious and more spartan scale, this is exactly what I did find, with a seated demon at the door, a child swathed in tartan, Pontius Pilate wearing a veil, and images of virgins with skulls. Was Bérenger Saunière enjoying a monumental spoof? Or was there something deeply significant about all of this?

How wonderfully susceptible to invention is the human mind. In 1956, two Frenchmen, Pierre Plantard and André Bonhomme, launched an association called the Prieuré de Sion, claiming that it was of ancient provenance. None other than Godefroi de Bouillon, the Crusader who in 1097 was offered, but declined, the crown of the Christian kingdom of Jerusalem, was said to have been the founder. At the same time, Plantard produced a manuscript and documents to prove that Father Saunière had indeed discovered something when he renovated St Maria Magdalena at Rennes-le-Château, and what he had discovered were parchments relating to the Merovingian line of Frankish kings under the protection of the Prieuré de Sion.

Then, as so often happens when someone creates a canard, he went too far. Plantard produced a comprehensive list of the priory's grand masters, which included the names of the great Renaissance painter and sculptor Leonardo da Vinci, the astrologer Michel de Notre-Dame (Nostradamus), the English scientist Isaac Newton, the writer Victor Hugo, the composer Claude Debussy and the surrealist film director Jean Cocteau, who had only recently died, but, had he lived, would no doubt have revelled in the accolade.[2]

The proposed goals of the Prieuré de Sion, Plantard announced, were the founding of a 'Holy European Empire' to become the next hyper-power dedicated to peace and prosperity, and the replacement of the Roman Catholic Church with an ecumenical messianic state. Derided by most, Plantard was nevertheless taken seriously by a small minority, including several writers of fiction. Pretty soon the Prieuré de Sion had gathered around it an enthusiastic cult following. It would seem that everyone, with the exception of the Catholic hierarchy, loves a wacky biblical intrigue. In 1991, Robert Plant, a member of the pop group Led Zeppelin, formed a breakaway band called the 'Priory of Brion', inspired by both the Prieuré de Sion and the controversial Monty Python film *The Life of Brian*.

Pierre Plantard died in Paris in 2000, but before that he had largely discredited himself by claiming that Roger-Patrice Pelat, a close friend of French president François Mitterrand, was at the centre of a financial scandal involving Pierre Bérégovoy, the French prime minister. Bérégovoy, claimed Plantard, was a former Grand Master of the Prieuré de Sion. As a consequence of this announcement, Pierre Plantard ended up in court, and when the judge ordered the police to conduct a search of his home, confessed to having made everything up, including the Prieuré de Sion. But who, in this complex world, can be certain he was telling the truth? Among the twenty-six names featured on Plantard's first list of former Grand Masters of the Prieuré de Sion are those of Marie de Saint-Clair and Jean de Saint-Clair, both having strong cognate connections with the family of Rosslyn.

As we are told by its inventor and followers, the avowed purpose of the Prieuré de Sion, the secret and durable command module of the Knights Templar, has been, throughout the centuries, to protect the descendants and rightful heirs of the Merovingian dynasty, the bloodline of Christ, the Holy Grail of *The Da Vinci Code*. If that dynasty is indeed today vested in the royal family of Great Britain, and if there is, as some modern Templars insist, a genuine historic connection between the twelfth-century Templars, the Prieuré de Sion, and the St Clairs of Rosslyn, can it be only a coincidence that Commander Peter Loughborough, 7th Earl of Rosslyn, inheritor of the ancient Barony of Rosslyn and owner of Rosslyn Castle and Rosslyn Chapel, should, in the year 2000, have been given specific responsibility for the protection of Her Majesty Queen Elizabeth II?

✠

SEVENTEEN

The Earls of Rosslyn

Keeping it in the family

O ne of the more intelligent aspects of the Scottish peerage
and honours system is that under the old Celtic tradition
it is usual for succession and titles to pass to the nearest
female and her progeny in the absence of an immediate male heir.
The reasoning behind this is simple. Since the mother carries the
child before birth, there is at least affirmation of the maternal
bloodline, if not that of the father. Not that this, in a world of
equal opportunities between the sexes, seeks to cast doubt upon
the long-established and widely endorsed practice of male primogeniture, but it does make sense when land is up for grabs or an
ancient title is in danger of extinction. It has always surprised me
that this eminently sensible ruling applies only to the Scottish
peerage and rarely to UK titles (such as dukedoms), unless under a
special remainder. It would have provided England with a far
greater sense of ancestral identity and continuity than today exists.

In 1778, when the last of the male St Clair bloodline of Rosslyn
died, only a modest inheritance passed to his only surviving
daughter, Sarah, who was married to Peter Wedderburn, a much
respected Edinburgh lawyer. When Wedderburn was made a
Judge of the Court of Session, he took the courtesy title of Lord
Chesterhall. They had a son and a daughter, Alexander and Janet,
and Alexander, having followed his father into the legal profession,
excelled all expectation. By 1762, when he prosecuted the

notorious Douglas Cause on behalf of the beautiful widowed
Duchess of Hamilton and her young son, Sir Alexander Wedderburn was considered to be one of the leading advocates of his
generation.

The Douglas Cause, the legal case which decided the future of
another great inheritance – lands, property and titles – following
the death of the first and last Duke of Douglas, rocked eighteenth-
century Hanoverian society both north and south of the Border.
When the Douglas estates were claimed by the late duke's
nephew, whose legitimacy was suspect – his mother, the duke's
sister, was over fifty when she gave birth to twins and it was alleged
that they were adopted – he was challenged by the family of his
kinsman the 7th Duke of Hamilton. To begin with, the Scottish
Court of Session ruled in favour of the Hamiltons' claim, but the
decision was overturned by the House of Lords.[1]

Sir Alexander Wedderburn had entered politics the previous
year and would become Lord Chancellor of Great Britain in the
Government of William Pitt. In 1780, he was raised to the
peerage as Lord Loughborough in the county of Surrey. In
1801 he took the title of 1st Earl of Rosslyn in recognition of
his mother's family. He died at his home in Windsor in 1805
following an attack of gout and was buried in St Paul's Cathedral
in London. Although married twice, the 1st earl had no children,
but such was the influence he exercised in an age when hereditary
status still stood for something that prior to his death he arranged
for all of his titles and inherited estates to pass to his nephew
Sir James St Clair-Erskine, the equally talented son of his sister,
Janet, who had married Sir Henry Erskine. Janet's mother-in-law,
Katherine Erskine, was, of course, General St Clair's youngest
sister, and therefore also their cousin. Sir James St Clair-Erskine,
who sat as MP for Kirkcaldy, was to crown his own career with the
rank of Lord President of the Council in Sir Robert Peel's Tory/
Whig coalition of 1834.

By any standards Alexander Wedderburn portfolio was substantial. In addition to property in England, there was Ravenscraig

Castle, 3,000 acres of land in Fife, and the equally prestigious, but by this stage rather neglected, Rosslyn Estate in Midlothian, which, along with Dysart House in Fife, reverted to the Rosslyn line of the family following the deaths of his great-uncle General Sir James St Clair and his cousin Colonel James Patterson.

As the nineteenth century moved forward, both Roslin Glen and the town itself acquired a further celebrity. Already a famed beauty spot, the gorge of the River North Esk and its surrounding woodlands were championed in the writings of the bestselling novelist Sir Walter Scott, who, in the early years of the century, was a resident at nearby Lasswade. When George IV visited Edinburgh in 1822, the first reigning British monarch to set foot on Scottish soil for over 200 years, Scotland was crying out for a sense of nationhood and found it not only in the mountains, glens and clans of the Highlands, but in the poetic landscape of the Scottish Lowlands. Rosslyn Chapel may now have become one of the great tourist destinations of the twenty-first century, but the Hanoverians and Victorians of two centuries ago also flocked here in their thousands, including, as one might have expected, Queen Victoria herself.

In 1842, at the very start of her first visit to Scotland, staying with the 5th Duke of Buccleuch at Dalkeith Palace, a short carriage drive away, she insisted on visiting Rosslyn Chapel, which she had heard so much about. She was so taken with what she saw on 14 September 1842 that she expressed a desire that 'so unique a gem be preserved for the country'. For better or worse, this opened the floodgates for Rosslyn as a tourist attraction.

By this stage, Lord Rosslyn had already commissioned the architect William Burn to begin repairs on the exterior. However, it would be a further twenty years before the interior of the chapel, possibly following a further nudge from Her Majesty, sprang to life again. In 1861, the 3rd Earl of Rosslyn was cajoled by his cousin by marriage, Lady Helen Wedderburn, daughter of the 7th Earl of Airlie, to reintroduce Sunday services. The architect David Bryce was summarily approached to begin the restoration work at a cost of £3,000. Flagstones were relaid in the crypt, a new altar was introduced, and the damaged carvings in the Lady Chapel were repaired. So as to offset some of the costs of the fixtures and fittings, the enterprising Lady Helen, who lived at Rosebank House on the estate, launched a subscription drive that was widely supported by the Scottish gentry far and wide.

Not everyone was happy though with the quality of the restoration work. One anonymous artist even went so far as to write to the *Scotsman* newspaper deploring the fact that the features which, in the eyes of his profession, rendered the chapel such an object of interest, of study and affection, were being lost forever. A similar reaction was sparked in certain quarters by the stone cleaning of Edinburgh's New Town at the end of the following century, but in the case of the chapel it seems to have largely been directed towards the 'uncalled for embellishments' imposed on some of the carvings.

Regardless of such controversy, Rosslyn Chapel was rededicated by Bishop Terrot of Edinburgh on Easter Tuesday, 22 April 1862, and formally reopened to the public with Bishop Forbes of Brechin preaching the first sermon. The Revd Cole, military chaplain at Greenlaw Barracks, near Penicuik, was constituted as Lord Rosslyn's domestic chaplain. Four years later, the 3rd earl was succeeded by his son who, in the years that followed, commissioned Andrew Kerr, a young architect, to create an apse to serve as a baptistery, with an organ loft above. A fine oak tracery displays the family crest, and in total, including Kerr's fees, the work cost the estate a substantial £792, the equivalent today of £46,000. The 4th earl's imposing tomb is situated in front of the baptistery entrance.

Any remainder of the original stained glass in the chapel windows had been destroyed during the Reformation, and for a long period of time there was no glass at all in the openings, the only protection being afforded by outside shutters. By the time of the 1862 restoration, however, they had been glazed with clear glass. Visiting Rosslyn Chapel today, therefore, it is important to understand that the jewel-like stained-glass windows in the Lady Chapel are of Victorian origin. In the six windows are the Twelve Apostles, their design created in 1867 for Francis, 4th Earl of Rosslyn, by Clayton & Bell of London, and dedicated to the memory of his parents.

In the east aisle are St John the Baptist with a lamb on a book, St Paul with a sword, St Mark and St Luke. The three windows of the north aisle feature images of the Annunciation and the Nativity, the Presentation in the Temple, the Baptism of Jesus, the Sermon on the Mount and the Miraculous Draught of Fishes. In the three windows of the south aisle are interpretations of the Miracle at the Marriage Feast of Cana, the Raising of Jairus's Daughter, Christ Blessing the Little Children, The Last Supper, the Crucifixion, and the Resurrection.

The east window, dedicated to the memory of the 4th earl's sister, Harriet, Countess of Derneburg in Hanover, shows the Resurrection of Our Lord. The west window features Our Blessed Lord in Glory. In 1887, the earl raised two further windows, one showing St George and the Dragon and dedicated to the memory of Andrew Kerr, who had supervised the building of the baptistery and since died; the second showing St Michael, inserted as a thanks offering from 'W. and H.A. Mitchell of Rosebank'.[2]

In his analysis of the 'meaning' of the chapel, the writer Tim Wallace-Murphy asks why two Roman soldiers, St Longinus, he who held the Spear of Destiny, and St Maurice, who was beheaded in front of his troops for refusing to worship the pagan gods of Rome, should be celebrated here? He also wonders why the patron saint of England is equally given his place, and makes a comparison with the mystical redecoration at the Church of St Maria Magdalena in Rennes-le-Château, which must have taken place around the very same time. Does this confirm that there is a connection between the two places of worship? Or is it just that what features there today is what was in vogue among certain factions of Christendom at the time? You either accept that the interiors of Rosslyn Chapel and St Maria Magdalena were comprehensibly brought about through the inventive imagination of independent scholars steeped in classical Christian and pagan mythology, or you take the view that some great transcendental master plan was at work. Either way, it provides a source of endless fascination.

However, thereafter you find yourself firmly implanted in the twentieth century, the windows in the baptistery dating only from 1954. These commemorate the current earl's uncle who died in active service during World War II, and his stepfather who died from injuries sustained during the same conflict. They were designed with a theme of the White Cliffs of Dover and St Andrew and St George. Another is dedicated to the 7th earl's grandmother, Princess Dmitri, and depicts St Francis of Assisi surrounded by birds and animals, including a kangaroo. Again this might cause any amount of curiosity should anyone be unaware that her family came from New South Wales.

✠

EIGHTEEN

Ley Lines and Energy Points

The Temple of Mithras

In common with the village of Rennes-le-Château, in France, Roslin, in Scotland, has been identified, by those who purport to know about such things, as straddling the meeting point of two sacred ley lines. Ley lines were officially 'rediscovered' by Alfred Watkins, a Herefordshire businessman, who in 1921 was perusing a map and noticed that a series of historical points of interest were situated upon a straight line. After much deliberation, his conclusion was that the entire world is connected with a series of mathematically regulated, invisible tracks that have a complex power in the ground and serve to link sacred places and natural magical sites.

Four years later he wrote a book on the subject, and thereafter his theories were taken up and expanded upon by several writers and notable New Age scientists, culminating in their being linked with UFO sightings and the ancient Chinese art of *feng shui*. As one might expect when one ventures into this kind of esoteric existentialism, it did not take long for somebody to claim that sudden upsurges of energy have, from time to time, been experienced within the village of Roslin and the nearby chapel.

The Revd Michael Fass, priest in charge of the congregation of St Matthew at Rosslyn Chapel, recalls standing before the transept when a visitor approached and angrily informed him that he was standing in her space. 'I did not have a clue what she was talking about!' he said. 'Was this not "our" space; the church in which we worship? And then she went on to say, "I have come a long way to stand on this spot where many ley lines meet, so please move over." ' The Revd Fass was unimpressed. 'That she should come into God's space and warn me off! Typical New Ager!'[1]

What serves only to excite this concept of a geometrical ground plan of the universe is the series of carvings of spirals, commonly known as 'cup' or 'ring' marks, to be found in Roslin Glen below the chapel. Some say that they too are representational of energy points on the surface of our plane of existence. Even a survey conducted by the Royal Commission on the Ancient and Historical Monuments of Scotland concludes that they are 'most unusual'. I was naturally intrigued by these markings in the glen which turned out, when I eventually managed to find them, to be a series of naive triangles, spirals and circles. To my eye they look aboriginal, but then my reaction, to say the least, is jaundiced. I hate to be a spoilsport, but in the same genre as the recurring fad for discovering crop circles, who is to prove that they were not the work of a local prankster?

Not so, according to the investigation conducted by VG Childe and John Taylor in 1938, and confirmed by Professor Breuil, co-author of *Rock Paintings of Southern Andalusia*. Childe and Taylor write that the techniques of their execution suggest the Hawthornden Scribings, as they describe them, should be added to the well-known series of memorials of Scottish Bronze Age art represented by 'cup-and-ring' markings. But, they caution, there are conspicuous differences, the most obvious being the complete absence of 'cups'. 'All the markings have been executed by pecking', they observed. 'We can detect no technical differences save in the quality of the rock, between the "alphabetical" signs (f and g) and the spirals and circles.'[2] Having established close stylistic affinities between the Irish Bronze Age and the conventional paintings of the Iberian peninsula, their conclusion is that these 'scribings' are of Irish origin, which does not sound nearly as exotic, but makes sense in the light of the early Celtic settlements which existed throughout Midlothian.

Online discussion occasionally takes place about these findings on the Internet, but I would firmly caution those considering further investigation. The necessary excursion involves crossing the River North Esk and climbing up a dangerous, muddy bank before even reaching anywhere close to where they are located. Even then, the patterns are exceedingly hard to see because the surfaces are largely covered over by moss or overhanging vegetation. To reach the shelf on which they lie requires a sensible degree of mountaineering skill.

Inevitably, Rosslyn does attract more than its fair share of oddballs. Staff in the chapel shop were recently alarmed when a man burst in and shouted out, 'Give me a match and I will burn the debts of the world!' The following day he was found making offerings on the altar, and it was later revealed that he had been sleeping rough in Wallace's Cave. 'You get used to it', I was told. 'Somebody once turned up claiming that he was the brother of Sarah Michelle Gellar, the girl who plays the lead in the American television series *Buffy the Vampire Slayer*. He wanted to know if there were any jobs going in the graveyard!'

Nonsense or not, there is definitely something about this place which consistently draws upon human sensitivities, in particular the great yearning shared by so many of us to find some inner truth as to what our existence is all about. More than one visitor has observed that what they have felt at Rosslyn, a sensation that it is not of this world, is undeniable. That it plays with the mind is obvious.

Another supposition, often voiced, is that the mound upon which the first St Clair castle, and later the chapel, was erected, was once the sacred centre of the kingdom of the ancient Picts, who also excavated the caves within the glen. It is also claimed that on this spot the Romans who invaded Scotland in or around the first and second century AD, built a temple, which they dedicated to Mithras, god of prosperity, lord of the skies, and judger of souls.

Mithras was the deity of the Roman soldiers dedicated to 'Duty'. He was worshipped in silence.

Some years ago, Niven Sinclair, founder member of the Friends of Rosslyn Chapel, who has dedicated his life to an investigation of his ancestor's creation, invited Professor Lun Yin, a prominent Buddhist, to accompany him on a tour, and claims to have been astounded by his reaction. Of all the temples and cathedrals the professor had been to see throughout the world, he said that he had never found anywhere with the same 'earth energy' as Rosslyn. He had brought with him a group of his followers, including several *feng shui* experts from Mongolia, Korea, Malaysia and Japan. Before they dispersed, it was suggested to Niven that the boundary wall to the east of the chapel, the one constructed by General Sir James St Clair in 1736, be forcibly removed, because it was preventing the ground energy from reaching into the chapel from the glen below. To date, this advice has been ignored.

In 1997, investigative holes were dug and one revealed an underground passageway leading from the chapel, under Gardener's Brae to Rosslyn Castle, which is some considerable distance away. At the time, the tunnel was described as being huge and very deep underground at the point where it enters under the chapel's foundations.

The steps that descend into the crypt from the main chapel end on a modern floor, but there is thought to be yet another flight of steep steps concealed beneath, leading in the opposite direction under the main building to a vault lying directly underneath the engrailed cross in the chapel roof. According to Niven, the passageway to begin with is 3 feet wide and 5 feet high where it emerges below the south door, its ceiling 8½ feet below ground level. After a straight run of approximately 25 feet, it turns 90 degrees towards the east and drops down the hillside with its roof 12½ feet below ground level. It then continues under the field towards the castle.

Fascinating though this discovery is, the Rosslyn Chapel Trust and Historic Scotland are now in general agreement that in future ground scans and similar investigations should not be carried out unless strictly necessary for conservation purposes. The consensus was that such interference would not only be damaging to the fabric of the chapel, but could prove detrimental to its reputation were there found to be nothing there. However, it is difficult to suppress the groundswell of curiosity that continues to envelope Rosslyn.

Secret passages and priest holes were commonplace in Catholic houses throughout Scotland, but coupled with the rumours of a lost treasure, secret societies, mediaeval knights, holy reliquaries, metaphysical goings on *and* the supernatural, is there anything left for Rosslyn to be associated with? Well, of course, there is always Gotham City, from the realms of comicbook fiction. In 1998, under the inspirational invention of writers Alan Grant and Frank Quitely, and courtesy of publishers DC Comics, the legendary caped crusader Batman, otherwise known as Bruce Wayne, descends upon the chapel to discover a hypnotic amulet hidden in a secret vault. All that is needed now is a visitation from Superman, Spiderman, Arnold Schwarzenegger and Austin Powers.

☦

NINETEEN

Downfall and Regeneration

Rosslyn's post-Reformation survival

rancis Robert St Clair-Erskine, 4th Earl of Rosslyn, was a
man of diverse talent. In 1878, Queen Victoria appointed
him her Ambassador Extraordinary to Madrid for the
marriage ceremony of King Alfonso XII to Princess Maria de
las Mercedes, daughter of the Duc de Montpensier. Sustained by
the immense income from his Fife coalmines, agricultural land
and other interests, he became a renowned breeder and trainer of
horses. In 1884, in an echo of the St Clair's ancestral connections
with Scotland's north-east coast, his daughter Millicent married
the 4th Duke of Sutherland and became mistress of the magnificent Dunrobin Castle at Golspie, in Sutherland.

It was an age of indulgence for the British upper classes, their
wealth and circumstances enabling them to fill their leisure time
with cultural pursuits of an amateur nature. Queen Victoria
herself painted in watercolours and published her diaries. Lord
Rosslyn was hailed as a poet of no small talent and ranked among
her favourites. When, in 1887, three years before his death, he
wrote a Jubilee Lyric entitled 'Love that Lasts Forever', it was
privately published by royal command. It can only be assumed
that this was of a more serious note than the one he wrote that is
quoted by his son, the 5th earl, in his memoirs: 'I kissed her till she
died of pain,/ and then I kissed her back to life again.'[1]

Alas, it appears that the noble lord was no more successful a businessman than he was a writer of ditties. In common with other race-going, landowning peers, notably the 5th Earl of Lonsdale, he lost a small fortune when he invested in cattle ranching in the American Midwest.[2] Despite this loss, at this stage, there was still plenty of money left. Indeed, he even went so far as to write to the ranching pioneer Moreton Frewin, whose scheme it had been, absolving him of blame.

An imposing red sandstone monument to the memory of the 4th earl, and his wife Blanche, stands, surmounted by a cross, on the lawn in front of the chapel's west-end baptistery door. It was carved by W Birnie Rhind, the Edinburgh-based sculptor, an appropriate choice given that it was he who created many of the figures on the Scott Monument and on the façade of the Scottish National Portrait Gallery. At the time of the 4th earl's death, despite the occasional poor investment, which in theory he could well afford, the bulk of the Rosslyn family fortune remained intact. By most standards, the Rosslyns could have been described as rich. That situation was about to undergo a drastic reversal.

Perhaps the 5th earl himself said it all with the title and content of his memoirs, *My Gamble with Life*, published in 1928, but whatever one might think of his profligacy, it is hard not to warm to his honesty and he was most certainly a survivor. All started well with his birth at Dysart House in 1864. At school in England, and throughout his teenage years, he was marked out as a precocious character, not always winning the approval of his father, but sons rarely do. At his wedding in London to Violet de Grey Vyner in 1890, the year of his father's death, the rites were performed by Rosslyn's chaplain, the Revd Thompson, and at the reception afterwards the Prince of Wales, later Edward VII, proposed the health of bride and groom.

The prince and the 5th earl became great friends, bonded through their love of racing, gambling and ladies of the stage. But living in the fast lane and keeping up with royalty comes at a cost. Lord Rosslyn was rarely rational with money, even when he no longer had any, and one of the greatest disasters to befall him was when he bet £15,000, a princely sum at the time, on his horse Buccaneer to win the Manchester Cup. Buccaneer lost. Six years after having come into a fortune, the 5th Earl of Rosslyn was declared bankrupt.

Selling Dysart House and its contents along with Ravenscraig Castle, he went to live at Home Farm at Balbeggie, in Fife, but that still did not cover his debts and he was soon estranged from his wife. When he finally sold the balance of his family's Fife coalmines in 1923, it saved him from penury, but the emotional cost was significant. 'It was for these coal-fields that we exchanged our rights to be kings of Orkney and Scotland,' he lamented miserably. Not one to give up easily, however, he became a stage actor, travelled the world as a journalist, and launched his own newspaper, *Scottish Life*. He married again, twice, and died in 1939, whereupon the earldom passed to his grandson, the father of the present, 7th, earl.

By this stage Rosslyn Chapel, although continuing as a place of worship, was starting to show visible signs of neglect. A report commissioned earlier in the century from the fashionable Fife-born architect Sir Robert Lorimer, six years after he had created the chapel of the Knights of the Thistle within St Giles' Cathedral, Edinburgh, recommended that the exterior of the roof, which was riddled with cracks, be covered over with asphalt. But greater, more fundamental forces were at work.

Unemployment during the late 1930s was widespread throughout Lowland Scotland. Money was scarce and public finances were stretched. In the early years of World War II, a letter of complaint was sent to the minister of labour reporting that the Scottish Episcopal congregation at Rosslyn Chapel on certain Sundays had dwindled to no more than two, and, given the cost of maintenance and heating, was it therefore appropriate for it to continue? To his eternal credit, Gwilym Lloyd George, a son of the World War I leader, then Minister of Fuel, responded by saying that he doubted that he would be able to justify such an economy of fuel in this world at the possible cost of a disproportionate expenditure of it on himself in the next!³

In the mid 1950s, Rosslyn Chapel's sacristy roof was further repaired, the carvings inside individually cleaned by hand. While the widespread and irresponsible demolition of old buildings was taking place throughout urban Britain, in rural communities 're-traditionalising' was suddenly in vogue. Unfortunately, this was something new and often the techniques employed were far from successful. Over the 1960s and 1970s, several buildings in the nearby New Town of Edinburgh, soot-grimed by decades of coal burning fires, were scrubbed and stone-blasted so as to become ten shades lighter, which certainly made them look better, but caused irreparable damage to the porous stone of their fabric. At Rosslyn Chapel too a solution of ammonia and water efficiently removed the surface grime, but the silica fluoride employed to seal the surfaces simply held in the damp. Of course, with the chapel gaining popularity as a venue for weddings and christenings, nobody realised what the consequences of water retention within the stone would be at the time.

In an era where almost every stately home in the land was throwing its doors open to the public, Rosslyn Chapel attracted its fair share of curiosity, especially following a visit from Her Majesty the Queen and the Duke of Edinburgh in 1966. The queen's sister, Princess Margaret, Countess of Snowdon, came in 1988. In 1993, the Friends of Rosslyn Chapel, spurred on by Niven Sinclair, and the artist Marianne Lines, organised a memorable afternoon and evening of events in memory of Prince Henry St Clair, and his epic voyage to America.

The Prince of Wales visited the chapel in 1998 and, always an admirer of mediaeval architecture, agreed to lend his support to the Rosslyn Development Project. His association with the family was further endorsed when, in 2003, he became patron of the Clan Sinclair Trust. More recently, the King and Queen of Sweden, accompanied by Baron St Clair Bonde, looked in during a private visit to Scotland.

In 1995, it was confirmed that the humidity in the chapel had become dangerously high, and urgent steps were required to restore the permeability of the richly carved inner surfaces. The trustees reacted promptly and within two years a purpose-built, free-standing steel structure was erected to encase the building under the supervision of leading Edinburgh-based architect James Simpson. Thus, the building as a whole is more watertight, enabling the roof vaults to dry outwards, away from the interior surfaces.

A second phase of restoration, supervised by James Simpson, began in 2000. Funded by the National Heritage Lottery Fund, the Eastern Scotland European Partnership, Historic Scotland, and the Rosslyn Chapel Trust, the east boundary walls were stabilised. A new roof of Caithness slate was erected over the existing crypt roof and the priest's cell, and two buildings of a later period beside the crypt were made functional.

In addition to this, the crypt staircase and the wooden screen at the west end were repaired, and the building totally rewired. Even more recently, it has been necessary to install a new entrance system, and to triple the size of the car park. The filming of *The Da Vinci Code* in September 2005, notwithstanding the funds that it generated towards the chapel's running costs, has led to the significant improvement of visitor facilities, not least the introduction of a more accessible interpretation centre.

✠

TWENTY

The Apprentice Pillar

Apocryphal or apocalyptic?

*D*uring the Edinburgh International Festival Fringe a group of players under the guise of Nonsense Room Productions annually enact the tale of *The Apprentice* written by Simon Beattie, a former tour guide at Rosslyn Chapel, and the son of Stuart Beattie, the chapel's custodian. The setting within the chapel is enchanting. The details are apocryphal; the moral, nevertheless, enduring. It comes as no surprise to find that the seats are sold out.

The plot to the story is thus: Rosslyn's master mason, having received instructions from his patron as to the design of an exquisite pillar, was hesitant to carry out the work until he had been to Rome for inspiration. While he was away, an apprentice, having seen the finished pillar in a dream, set about the work. When the master mason returned he was so jealous of his apprentice's achievement that he murdered the young man in a fit of rage.

For aficionados of the initiation rituals of Freemasonry, it probably sounds familiar. Hiram Abiff was the principal architect of the Temple of Solomon. There were large numbers of master masons employed in the building of the temple, but only King Solomon, the King of Tyre, and Hiram Abiff, the son of 'a widow of the tribe of Naphtali', shared the secrets of the High and Sublime Degree. As a result, when certain craftsmen sought to further their knowledge, they approached Hiram and, when he refused to help them, murdered him in the manner described in Masonic ritual.

Thus, with the relentless passage of time, do legends become intermingled, adapted and elaborated upon. Furthermore, in 1893, the Revd Thompson tells us that similar legends existed at Melrose Abbey, and the cathedrals of Lincoln and Rouen, implying that these masons must have been a fiercely competitive bunch, especially when it came to storytelling.[1]

Not only is the tale of the Rosslyn apprentice not unique to Rosslyn, it is further undermined by the column in question having previously been referred to as the Prince's Pillar. Those who are determined to perpetuate the legend point to the image known as the 'Apprentice Carving' situated about halfway up the west wall of the choir, on the south side. This shows a face with a deep scar on the right temple. Leering on the opposite corner is the head of his murderer, the master. These carvings, it is claimed, were designed to commemorate the incident, but again this is pure conjecture. Moreover, Father Hay makes no mention of it.

Notwithstanding all this, the Apprentice or Prince's Pillar, on the south-east of the choir, in close proximity to the steps leading to the crypt, remains one of the most aesthetically crafted architectural features of all time, surpassing all of the others within the chapel. In his booklet *The Templar Legacy and The Masonic Inheritance Within Rosslyn Chapel*, Tim Wallace-Murphy observes that it represents 'the Yggdrasil tree of Norse mythology, the World Ash which binds together Heaven, Earth and Hell. The crown of the "tree" comprises the twelve constellations of the Zodiac. The spiralling branches symbolise plants and the roots of the trunk dig deeply into the elements of the Earth. At the bottom of the pillar the dragons of Neilfelheim can be seen gnawing at the roots of the tree to rob it of its fruitfulness.'

Certainly, the carvings appear to depict only leaves, pointing to it being symbolic of the Tree of Life, which is probably exactly what was intended, given that much of the inspiration for the carvings throughout originates from the Old or New Testaments, in this case either the Book of Genesis or the Book of Revelation. Of course, it cannot be ignored that the Tree of Life also features in several pagan religions and in Kabbalah, the tradition of Jewish mysticism, but there are limits to the fifteenth-century knowledge of even Prince William St Clair and his stone carvers. Notwithstanding, a more recent and even more esoteric claim is that the coiled spirals that encircle the pillar are an early representation of the double helix of DNA. No doubt we will hear considerably more on this thesis in years to come.

Behind the altar, in front of the Lady Chapel, and to the left of the Apprentice Pillar, are two other remarkable load-bearing columns. The first, under the east window, is known as the Mason's Pillar; the one in the centre, the Journeyman's Pillar. Although the former is a work of intricate tracery, the second is a testament to simplicity and equally pleasing to the eye. But there is an anomaly here. In none of the surviving pictorial representations of the Mason's Pillar painted prior to David Bryce's restoration work of the early 1860s (for examples see *The Apprentice Pillar, Rosslyn Chapel* by George Shepherd after Joseph Gandy, 1809, in the Victoria and Albert Museum, London, or Samuel Dickinfield Swarbreck's *Lady Chapel, Rosslyn Chapel*, 1837) does the heavily tooled decoration on its central panels appear. The conclusion is that it is, in all likelihood, a Victorian embellishment, and no doubt a serious contributor to the controversy that surrounded the repair work (see Chapter 17). Certainly the tracery was in place when the chapel was photographed by George Washington Wilson in 1880.[2]

Questions of restoration aside, what elevates these pillars and enhances their beauty still further – and indeed that of all of the columns encapsulating the choir – are the carvings on the ceiling above them. The sheer quantity of illustration is blinding, the beauty of the whole distracting from the biblical storylines within the detail: the Fall of Man and Expulsion from Eden, the Dance of Death, the Birth of Christ, the Sacrifice of Isaac, the Victory of Truth, the Contrast between Virtue and Vice, the Annunciation, the Presentation of Christ in the Temple, Jesus the Carpenter, the Prodigal feeding the Swine, the Crucifixion and Descent from the Cross, the Resurrection and Rolling Away of the Stone from the Holy Sepulchre, the Conquest over Death, and Our Lord Seated in Glory. But this is no preachy, intolerant place. Interspersed throughout is the humour. Wit and wisdom go hand in hand.

What strikes me as the most fascinating aspect of all is the sheer dazzling intensity of visible spiritual and academic thought that has gone into it. Bear in mind that these images were created more or less around the same time as William Caxton first introduced the printed word into England. Up until then, only handwritten manuscripts had existed in the West. Many were beautifully 'illuminated' with gilt and coloured embellishment, but few manuscripts of any description were in wide circulation. The Holy Roman Church was considered, and considered itself, to be the font of all knowledge, but the paradox of Rosslyn Chapel, erected to glorify the teachings of that very Church, is that almost every spiritual influence which existed in the centuries before it was conceived are illustrated on its walls and ceilings: Greek, Babylonian, Egyptian, Hebrew and pagan Norse.

And remember that all of this was created in mediaeval Scotland. Although St Andrews University had been in existence for over thirty years when the chapel was built, the universities of Glasgow and Aberdeen were only in the early stages of being set up. The Renaissance thinking of mainland Europe had only just begun to infiltrate the British Isles, a cultural backwater compared to Italy, where, in Milan, a young painter called Leonardo da Vinci was about to embark upon *The Last Supper*. His future rival, Michelangelo di Lodovico Buonarroti Simoni, was an adolescent living in Caprese in Tuscany, where his father was mayor. Within this context, the stone decoration of Rosslyn Chapel can be seen as a breathtaking tribute to the scholarly genius of Prince William St Clair and the team of carvers whom he employed. Taken in its entirety, it ranks among the most outstanding and miraculous achievements of the second millennium.

TWENTY-ONE

✠

Religious Symbolism and Underworld Messaging

Decoding the stones

*W*ithin the interiors of Rosslyn Chapel are carved decorations in stone which are inspired by virtually every spiritual influence in existence before and during the period in which the chapel was built: Greek, Babylonian, Egyptian, Hebrew, pagan Norse and Pict. The barrel-vaulted roof is dotted with images of stars, lilies, and roses. There are carvings of the constellations of the Zodiac, dragons, the orb of the sun, and the engrailed cross of the St Clairs. All of this amounts to one vast puzzle, taxing the brains of anyone who so much as casts a glance in their direction. How much more pleasant it is simply to absorb the whole in all its delicate, cluttered beauty without finding any necessity to question its purpose.

When Dorothy Wordsworth visited the chapel with her brother William, the English Romantic poet, in 1803, she observed of the ceiling that the whole of the groundwork upon which the leaves and flowers were delicately wrought was stained by time with the softest colours: 'Some of those leaves and flowers were tinged perfectly green, and at one part the effect was most exquisite – three or four leaves of a small fern, resembling that which we call Adder's Tongue, grew round a cluster of them at the top of a pillar, and the natural product and the artificial were so intermingled that, at first, it was not easy to distinguish the living plant from the other.'[1] Such was the triumph of nature and art working in perfect harmony. The staining of years of damp and algae, however, was not to be tolerated, especially as the chapel was gradually developing into a popular tourist venue as the word spread. By the time of Queen Victoria's visit forty years on, the bulk of the damage created by the elements had been rectified to shades of cream and silken white, a matrix for the flashes of vivid colour – amber, azure, scarlet and gold – cast by the sun through stained glass.

To attempt to understand the mind of Prince William St Clair, and those of the craftsmen he employed, would take a lifetime if you choose to look for motives where there are none, beyond simple decoration. After all, there is always the possibility that the illustrations which feature within the chapel might, in the final analysis, amount to nothing more than random choice. The problem is that the later centuries of the second millennium have been gripped with an uncomfortable, often unrewarding, obsession with answers. Were Prince William able to listen to some of the wilder fables that have been concocted around his invention, I am sure that he would be laughing out loud in his mediaeval stockings.

While a great deal of speculation therefore surrounds the hidden meaning of the imagery to be found at Rosslyn, it is often overlooked that they present us with another mystery. As noted in the preceding chapter, these carvings were manufactured at a time when knowledge was exclusive to a small, scholarly elite, one that was for the most part entrenched within the confines of the mother Church. Quite where and how Prince William came by so much information from so many different, and sometimes conflicting, influences is just as baffling as the choice of motifs themselves.

The historical context of the chapel throws up other points of interest too. The interiors of Rosslyn Chapel were created in mediaeval Scotland, a land of bleak fortification and plain stone, although the abbeys of Melrose, Dryburgh, Dundrennan and Glasgow Cathedral do stand out as beacons within this general-isation. Yet this was the same period when the intelligentsia of Renaissance Italy was rallying to the genius of Piero Della Francesca, Giovanni Bellini, and the younger Raffaello Santi. It has to be understood therefore that Scotland was enjoying its own short-lived Renaissance, added to which were these stone carvings of such an unprecedented quality and inventive inter-pretation that it would be some time before they were matched elsewhere.

Although history lauds its patrons of the arts, its discerning men and women of wealth and prominence, the craftsmen who actually produce the work for them are often overlooked. At Rosslyn Chapel during the late fifteenth century great minds were at work, but unfairly such talents were doomed to remain anonymous. How often have you found yourself complimenting the owners of a stylish home on how clever they have been to create such elegance and style when all that they have done is to approve an architect's design, choose an interior decorator and write a large cheque? That is why a certain sympathy should be felt for those anonymous masons of Rosslyn Chapel although, un-usually for the period, some of them did leave their marks, their personal footprints in the sand. Posterity will never know their names, but what they created, in the words of John Ritchie, whose grandfather was caretaker of the chapel and castle during World War II, is a visual series of writings in stone. 'Rosslyn was a scriptorium,' he says. He is convinced that original manuscripts relating to the Bible and on loan from the Church were copied under the watchful eye of Sir Gilbert Hay, who was Prince William's tutor, and their storylines later perpetuated in stone.

'There is a great deal to be seen outside to excite wonder and admiration: much that is grotesque and amusing', wrote the Revd Thompson in 1893, noting the gargoyles over the porch on the north side. Nearby there is a man with pointed ears;

another holds a stick between his arms and legs; a figure is shown in pursuit of a fox with a goose. But neither religious fanaticism, nor Scotland's weather, nor, indeed, the well-meaning conservation schemes of the past century have been kind to the chapel's exterior stonework. The most remarkable achievement of all is that so much has survived regardless.

To embark upon a study of the carvings within Rosslyn Chapel, however, is to set forth upon a journey through even wilder flights of the imagination. If there is any criticism that can be made, it is that the sheer density of illustration on display is bewildering and detracts from the genius of the detail. But who can tell that this was not intentional? The more quirky motifs appear dangerously sacrilegious for a House of God. Interspersed within the mainstream decoration is a network of insurgency. For example, there are approximately 120 carvings of the Green Man, the most potent Celtic symbol of fertility and rebirth,[2] showing man's progression through the four seasons. Spring is represented by a youth on the east wall; the same face is transformed by maturity into manhood, then into the corpulent features of autumn on the west wall. The sequence culminates with a skull, symbolic of the arrival of winter.

In bold contrast to its pagan symbols are groupings of religious allegories depicting the Seven Acts of Mercy, the Seven Deadly Sins, and the Dance of Death. Whoever chose these storylines for illustration was possessed of a formidable scholarly intellect. Far be it for this humble writer to dismiss the genius of Prince William as the originator, but from the sheer density of ideas apparent within such themes, it seems that he must have had the support of an impressively well-educated and inventive team. Remember again that this was long before the widespread distribution of the printed word or even handwritten manuscript. Besides, the ability to read was restricted to only a minority.

Such handwritten copies of the Scriptures as existed were written in Latin and jealously kept within the confines of the orthodox Church authorities. Printing, it should be understood, was first introduced into Scotland by Bishop Elphinstone in 1507, the first Scottish press being established by Andrew Myllar of Edinburgh. The New Testament was first translated from Latin into English by William Tyndale as late as 1526. Whoever they were, these anonymous artists and stonemasons of Rosslyn Chapel, the knowledge they shared in the absence of written instruction is truly breathtaking.

As one enters the choir from the baptistery the most dazzling feature is the ceiling high above – held up on either side by windows and literally squared off into ten sections – which features cut-out daisies, lilies, flowers, roses and stars. Angels stand guard over the entrance below: one with a sword, another in prayer. Each block of the ceiling design is original, with minimal restoration: one has a moon and a star; another shows a dove with outspread wings; a sun hovers over an outstretched hand. Suspended from a rib projecting downwards, a pair of hands holds the shield of the St Clairs embossed with its engrailed cross. The statue of the Virgin Mary rises above the principal altar at the east end, a Victorian replacement for whatever stood here before the desecration of the Reformation.

Much of the original statuary is thought to have been destroyed by those Protestant wreckers in 1688, but Baron St Clair Bonde is not convinced. 'Had the statuary been destroyed, then some of the plinths would have been damaged in the process', he says. 'This is not the case. All the plinths remain perfectly intact. I also suspect that had the statuary been totally destroyed, then there would be pieces of it discovered lying around somewhere in the neighbourhood.'

The venom of the mob was concentrated on the Catholic idolatry within the chapel, and hence the majority of more obscure carving has survived intact. Whether some statues were spirited away before the mob's arrival, we will never know, but a more likely possibility is that the more valuable and moveable effigies were secreted away in the vaults. In mediaeval times everything would have been brightly painted in order for the images to stand out, but not so that which remains, the colour having faded over the centuries. In their 21st-century preserved state, virtually everything has been left uncoloured in virginal relief, although there are a few carvings which have been lightly coloured to put them into their original context.

To the right, facing the altar, is a pillar above which there is a lion and a unicorn in combat. Immediately above the unicorn's head, stretching over to the neighbouring pillar, are figures representing the twelve apostles and four martyrs, all with halos over their heads. On the north aisle stands the Caithness Tomb which displays the Caithness coat-of-arms and the family motto: 'Commit the Verk to God'. This was erected in memory of the 4th earl, great-grandson of the chapel's founder. On the pinnacle of the arch which surmounts it is the carving of an artichoke.[3] Quite what one should read into that is anyone's guess.

Upright against the same wall is the burial stone of Sir William St Clair who was killed by the Moors at Teba in Andalucia while seeking to transport the heart of King Robert I to the Holy Land. This event took place over 116 years before the building of the chapel began and the stone was allegedly brought here by General St Clair in 1736, having removed it from the ruins of the earlier church thought to have stood in the vicinity of the village graveyard. What further adds to the intrigue of this slab is that it shows the outline of a Highland sword, and beside it a floriated cross on a long flute. Carved next to the stem is the name Willhm de Sinncler. At the end of the stone are the letters ER, one above the other. Why a Highland sword? Does this connect him with the Templars of Kilmartin, whose burial slabs are remarkably similar? And what do the initials ER stand for? Again, there are more questions than answers.

Everywhere, throughout the chapel, there are numerous angels carrying scrolls: one holds a seal; another wears a skull cap and holds a heart. Nearby, the jaws of a lion are being forcibly held open, possibly a reference to Daniel in the lions' den. To the left of this is an elephant. Further along the same aisle, an architrave above the pillars features eight figures. Seven have crowns upon their heads. The one in the middle has his hands outstretched above him. One of them clutches a harp. In the Lady Chapel are scenes from the Nativity – the Virgin and Child and the Three Wise Men. More angels are in evidence here, singing and playing musical instruments.

Prince William valued his musicians. As previously mentioned, a pathway leading downhill from the chapel to the castle is still known as the Minstrels Walk. One of the angels holds a set of bagpipes. This provides us with another conundrum since the exact origin of the bagpipes, now so strongly associated with Scotland, has never been determined. Seemingly they arrived with the Celts, but similar instruments existed in the Middle East several centuries before the birth of Christ. By the mid fourteenth century, however, they were commonplace throughout Scotland, so the inspiration behind this figure was probably local. However, a carving of a pig playing the bagpipes can also be seen at Melrose Abbey and, in the early twentieth century, inspired a similar image within the Thistle Chapel in St Giles' Cathedral in Edinburgh.

Another angel within the Lady Chapel demands special attention. He or she is upside down and roped around the middle. Some say this represents Lucifer, the fallen angel. Close by, another holds a scroll, and there is the moulding of a face, said to have been taken from the death mask of Robert the Bruce. On a ribbed arch there are sixteen figures accompanied by skeletons to symbolise the 'dance of death', a popular mediaeval preoccupation to remind us that 'in the midst of life we are in death'.

As has been previously observed, all kinds of plant life are visible: oak leaves, flowers, fern and kale, and a myriad of roses and sunflowers.

An eccentric inscription, in Lombardic lettering, presumably being the mother tongue of its writer, reads 'Forte est vinu. Fortior est rex. Fortiores sunt mulieres: sup om vincit veritas', which translates as 'Wine is strong. The king is stronger. Women are stronger still: but truth conquers all.' This quote, originating from 1 Edras (Ezra after the Reformation) in the Old Testament, was used to test the three bodyguards of Darius, King of Persia, around 538 BC. The winner was Zerubbabel, from the line of David. In return for his wisdom, Zerubbabel was told that he could have anything he liked, and he therefore asked that the Jews might return to Jerusalem to rebuild their temple.

What immediacy did such words, the only quotation to feature in the chapel, have for Prince William St Clair? Do not forget that this was a man who in his lifetime had three wives and fathered at least eighteen children. Or might it be, as has been suggested, a coded reference to something infinitely more potent? A message of such profundity that when its meaning is ultimately revealed it will shake mankind?

Niven Sinclair, founder member of the Friends of Rosslyn Chapel, has written astutely on this subject and points out that at right angles to the quotation is a figure thought to represent the sleeping King Darius, and that he is being watched over by two young bodyguards, not three. What has become of the third bodyguard, wonders Sinclair. Did too much wine cause him to fall? Everyone loves a paradox.

From this same point in the south aisle can be seen illustrations of moral rectitude: helping the needy, clothing the naked, looking after the infirm, a man carrying bags of money, presumably to hand out to the poor, somebody feeding the starving, and somebody burying the dead. A line-up of the deadly sins features a Pharisee with puffed-out chest for pride, a man with a pitcher in his mouth for gluttony, a man with an axe and a club for anger, a man surrounded by grapes for envy, someone pulling unenthusiastically at a sack for sloth, and lovers in an embrace for lust. Just to add to the complexity, 'avarice', which belongs to the sins on one side, has been transposed with 'charity' from the virtues on the other.

An angel holds what must surely be the heart of Robert the Bruce. There is Moses with a horned head. In Exodus 34, verse 29, the face of Moses is described in Hebrew as being 'radiant'; the Hebrew word for radiant is *karan*, similar to the Hebrew word for horn, which is *karen*. The mediaeval idea that Moses was horned came about when the original Hebrew was translated into Latin.

The Ten Commandments are also depicted. A small carving of St Veronica holds a veil upon which is an image of the head of Jesus. This has been associated with the Turin Shroud, a centuries-old linen cloth which bears the image of a crucified man whom millions believe to be that of Jesus of Nazareth himself. The shroud was first mentioned around the year 1360, and nearly lost in a fire in 1532. Today it is kept in the cathedral of St John the Baptist in Turin, but its authenticity has been widely discredited. A parallel legend is that of the veil upon which Jesus wiped his brow. When it was returned to its owner, St Veronica, the Saviour's features were impregnated upon the cloth. The alleged original can be inspected at St Peter's in Rome.

Next we find a tribute to the founder's ancestor, William the Seemly, shown as a knight on horseback carrying a spear. Behind him is a figure holding the Holy Rude. Such images inevitably conjour up links with the Knights Templar who over the centuries have enjoyed more than their fair quota of symbols, many of them absorbed into Freemasonry: the skull and crossbones, two doves in flight, trowels and compasses etc. For anyone to suggest, however, that there is a hidden agenda to be found in the carving of two men mounted on the same horse is not dissimilar to claiming that Templar symbolism is to be found in the 1969 hit song 'Two Little Boys' sung by Rolf Harris.

Every carving in Rosslyn Chapel must be regarded as an individual work of art and judged on its own merit. Each and every one of us can find something here either to admire or to tease. Every image is in itself unique, but drowned in the quantity and quality of its companions. Perhaps this explains how a tiny mediaeval Scottish church has so successfully survived the more violent excesses it has witnessed through time: by baffling the intruders with the sheer intensity of its creation and by denying them an absolute understanding of the detail.

☨

TWENTY-TWO

A Place of Pilgrimage

The impact of tourism

O ral tradition has it that as many as seventeen of the St Clair barons of Rosslyn are interred beneath the floor of Rosslyn Chapel, all of them encased in their suits of armour. In *The Lay of the Last Minstrel*, Sir Walter Scott claims that there are twenty. John Slezer's *Theatrum Scotiae*, published in the seventeenth century, refers to three princes of Orkney, and nine St Clair barons, a total of twelve. My personal confirmation of this, although not the exact number of knights concerned, came during a visit to Edinburgh University several years ago.

I was on an entirely different mission, researching an article on industrial land surveying, when I was called over to examine some print-outs from a seismic survey which had taken place at the chapel on the previous day. Clearly showing up blue against the thin black outlines on the paper were several objects situated deep within the foundations. The importance of this initiative, which is described in Andrew Sinclair's *The Sword and the Grail*, was that it to some extent, but by no means conclusively, confirmed the theme of Sir Walter Scott's *The Lay of the Last Minstrel*, published in 1805:

> Seem'd all on fire that chapel proud
> Where Roslin's chiefs uncoffin'd lie
> Each Baron, for a sable shroud,
> Sheathed in his iron panoply.

As a friend of the St Clair family, Sir Walter would doubtless have been aware of Father Hay's manuscript from a century earlier in which he so vividly describes the opening of the airless vaults for the interment of his stepfather, Sir James, first of the dynasty to be encased in a coffin, since his wife considered the practice of burial without one as being barbaric. As his stepfather's casket was being installed, however, the funeral party came across the armour-suited body of Sir James's grandfather:

His corpse [that of Sir William St Clair] seemed to be entire at the opening of the cave; but when they came to touch his body, it fell into dust. He was lying in his armour, with a red velvet cap on his head, on a flat stone; nothing was spoiled except a piece of the white furring that went around his cap, and answered to the hinder part of the head. All his predecessors were buried after the same manner, in their armour. Late Rosaline, my good father, was the first that was buried in a coffin against the sentiments of King James the Seventh, who was then in Scotland, and several other persons well versed in antiquity, to whom my mother would not hearken, thinking it beggarly to be buried after that manner.

'It wasn't all that unusual to be buried in your suit of armour,' explained the author and historian AJ Stewart during our visit to the chapel in the summer of 2005. 'It was partly to do with the preservation of the flesh. If you had been well embalmed before being clapped around in steel so that the worms couldn't get at you, it was rather like being tinned. Besides, it was much more hygienic. If you were buried in armour, you were protected from the wrath of Heaven and the worms of Hell.'

That there were metallic objects in the vaults of Rosslyn Chapel I can certainly confirm from my brief inspection of those ground scans all that time ago, but the evidence that these were suits of armour appears to be contradicted by the 5th Earl of Rosslyn, the actor, who, in 1899, while appearing as Sir Walter Raleigh in a production of *Kenilworth* staged in Edinburgh and Glasgow, took time off for an investigation of his own.[1] 'In the presence of a well-known antiquary, we removed the stone lids of three or four of the vaults,' he writes in his memoirs. 'That they [the knights] were buried without coffins was true, but we found no traces of armour, though I did not pursue my search through the tombs.' Which, of course, poses the question as to what happened to those suits of armour, and what exactly was I looking at on those computer print-outs?

To date, the catacombs, the vaults, or whatever the foundations of Rosslyn Chapel are concealing, remain unexplored and in my opinion, rightly so. Following the ground scans, an attempt was made to penetrate the lower vaults with core drillers. The team was led by Andrew Sinclair, who lowered an industrial endoscope through a tube, in the hope that it would reveal all. No such luck. All they found was 10 feet of rubble, and, having cut through to the upper vault roof, they found that this consisted of 3 feet of solid stone. After a week of fruitless endeavour, they gave up.

Historic Scotland, the Government organisation that safeguards Scotland's built heritage, and seeks to promote its understanding and enjoyment, has taken the stance that any further intrusive investigation would be detrimental to the chapel's long-term wellbeing. The trustees concur. Furthermore, since graves are involved, the legal Right of Sepulchre, which protects the burial grounds of the dead from desecration, would first have to be revoked. Let the dead rest in peace, I say.

So we may never know what, if anything, is hidden in the depths below Rosslyn's choir and this is I think as it should be in the great scheme of things. Imagine, for example, the reaction there would be if a major excavation was to take place and nothing was found. Yet there are other compelling diversions to dwell upon. Rosslyn's mystical attraction is not solely focussed on hidden treasure; far from it. Sir Walter Scott's melancholy verses from *The Lay of the Last Minstrel* continue to resonate:

O Listen, listen ladies gay!
No haughty feat of arms I tell
Soft is the note, and sad the lay
That mourns the lovely Rosabelle.

O'er Roslin all that dreary night
A wondrous blaze was seen to gleam;
'Twas broader than the watch-fire's light,
And redder than the bright moon-beam.

It glared on Roslin's castle rock,
It ruddied all the copse-wood glen,
'Twas seen from Dryden's groves of oak,
And seen from caverned Hawthornden.

Who was the lovely Rosabelle, so tragically drowned in the Firth of Forth on her way to Rosslyn, for whom a fire, natural or supernatural, was said to burn above the castle? As with so much of the history of Rosslyn, there are differing interpretations of this story, none of them conclusive, and no one has been able to identify exactly who she was.

The 5th Earl of Rosslyn writes that Henry St Clair, the twelfth-century Crusader, was engaged to Rosabelle, daughter of the Earl of Strathmore, which is unlikely since the earldom of Strathmore was only created in 1677. A misprint? Or a red herring? The St Clair family tree lists this Sir Henry's wife as Rosabelle Forteith, daughter of Malise, 1st Earl of Strathearn. In a recent 'families and local histories' survey of the ancestors of HRH Prince William, heir to the British throne, this good lady was listed as his twenty-five times' great aunt. However, with so little record kept, and so much of the relevant documentation destroyed (in the Rosslyn Castle fire of 1447, and General Monck's attack of 1650), I would suggest that it is virtually impossible to work this one out for certain.

It is therefore not at all surprising that a certain amount of confusion surrounds the links between the St Clairs and the earls of Strathearn, especially since their families entwine in at least three generations. Rosabelle, daughter of the 1st Earl of Strathearn, married Henry St Clair in the early twelfth century. Katherine, daughter of the 4th earl, married another Henry St Clair in around 1200. In the fourteenth century, Isabella, daughter of the 8th earl, married William St Clair, the union through which their son, yet another Henry, acquired the Orkney earldom.

Sir Walter's ballad tells us that the 'lovely Rosabelle', was at Ravensheugh (Ravenscraig) Castle on the coast of Fife on the day that a ball was to be held at Rosslyn Castle. For a start, this has to have been Sir Walter's invention since Ravenscraig Castle was yet to be built and only became a St Clair possession in the late fifteenth century. Continuing regardless, it seems it was a stormy afternoon and, seeing distant lights across the Firth of Forth, the lady in question was seized with a great yearning to see the handsome Lord Lindesay's heir, who was to be a guest at the ball. Although previously warned not to travel by a seer, who prophesied 'a wet shroud' for the 'ladye gay', the lovely Rosabelle persuaded some reluctant fishermen to row her across the estuary. Alas, her barge soon encountered blackening waves and tragically all were drowned.

In the words of Sir Walter Scott, Rosabelle's reasons for going were thus:

> 'Tis not because Lord Lindesay's heir
> To-night at Roslin leads the ball,
> But that my ladye-mother there
> Sits lonely in her castle-hall
>
> 'Tis not because the ring they ride
> And Lindesay at the ring rides well,
> But that my sire the wine will chide
> If 'tis not filled by Rosabelle.

My personal opinion is that the lovely Rosabelle was neither Sir Henry's fiancée nor wife, but his daughter, otherwise it is unlikely she would have been expected to be on hand to pour the wine, and her interest in Lord Lindesay's heir would appear, would it not, a trifle inappropriate?

With regard to the chapel being 'on fire', it has been suggested that this is simply a recognition of the St Clair family's Norse origins and the Viking ritual of cremation at sea. Illusions of fire and flame in the sky are commonplace throughout Scottish history, the most notable example dating from 1689, when a red glow was reported over the Perthshire landscape on the eve of the Battle of Killiecrankie. At Rosslyn, the tradition survives that whenever a member of the immediate family is about to die, the windows of Rosslyn Castle are lit up by the setting sun. This is certainly what the 5th earl claims he was told when his grandfather expired at Dysart in 1866.

Personally, I love these old Scottish legends. Whenever a Duke of Hamilton dies, a white stag is said to appear at Brodick Castle on Arran. The Haigs of Bemersyde are forewarned by a headless horseman. The sound of drums precedes the death of an Ogilvie of Airlie and, according to the late Sir Iain Moncreiffe, the death of a Lord Herries is heralded by the arrival of hedgehogs upon his ancestral lawn.

✠

TWENTY-THREE

Rosslyn in the Third Millennium

Faith endures

*V*iewed from any angle and distance, with the roof of the chapel visible on the hill above or beyond, Rosslyn Castle today suggests a Disney-esque amalgamation of Camelot and a Jane Austen villa, its sides dropping precariously into the glen far below. You could easily imagine a family of JRR Tolkien's hobbits being in residence here, or one of those necromancer lairds of the Scottish Border ballads.

Turning sharply on to the low road at the south end of Roslin village, a slope snakes languidly downhill, looping and rising steeply to eventually connect with the A6094 close to Rosewell. Since this is an unexpectedly busy and rather narrow route, it is inadvisable to stop if you are driving. However, seen from across the blanket of trees from the south and from the east, the castle grouping becomes a fantasy high-rise from some melancholy mediaeval fable. You might almost expect to see a 'Here be Dragons' signpost.

Yet from the front entrance, on the far side and accessed by a bridge over the glen, the aspect is entirely different. The façade of the main dwelling house within the front courtyard is enclosed by the ruinous remains of the fifteenth-century gatehouse, and cordoned off by a hedge. A sixteenth-century gateway to the northern range was modified in 1690. Also in evidence are the remnants of the late fifteenth-century west range, a rectangular-plan tower, a 1597-built east curtain wall tower, and a range modified in 1622. The approach to this courtyard is over a fifteenth-century bridge, largely reconstructed in 1597. The fabric is pink sandstone rubble. The main dwelling, which appears unexpectedly modern among its ruined surroundings, has slate roofs. Windows are sash, casement or fixed, some with astragals.[1]

From the muddy footpath below the causeway bridge, a stark rock face soars bleakly upwards. A popular belief has it that the Devil himself rode a black horse vertically up this precipice. Look closely. The hoofprints are still visible.

It is almost one thousand years since William St Clair, known as 'the Seemly', was granted these lands of Rosslyn by a legendary Scottish king and his saintly Saxon wife. What is all the more remarkable is that his kenspeckle descendants have succeeded in hanging on to their inheritance through siege and battle, religious strife and erosive death duties, a common bane of the British aristocracy. To achieve this, they have simply moved with the times.

Their castle today, whilst remaining in the ownership of the 7th Earl of Rosslyn, is let out through the Landmark Trust, a charity founded in 1965 which rescues and restores historic buildings at risk and makes them available for holiday lettings. Rosslyn Chapel is conserved and opened to the public by the Rosslyn Chapel Trust, which holds it on 99-year lease from the Rosslyn family. The Rosslyn Chapel Trust has ambitious plans for the comprehensive repair of the chapel, securing its long-term future, and for a sensitive new building to welcome visitors and introduce them to the history and architecture of the chapel. In addition, the trust encourages the use of the chapel by the Scottish Episcopal Church.

Thanks to Scotland's Celtic tradition in which inheritance favours the female line in the absence of an immediate male heir, the family titles of the St Clairs too have passed through the generations relatively intact. Thus we find the earldoms of Caithness and Rosslyn, and the lordship of Sinclair, extant, with the more ancient lordship of St Clair in the process of being reinstated in the Scottish–Swedish Bonde family of Fife.

Have a look on the Internet and, at my last count, there are 5,630,000 websites connected with the name of St Clair, and 7,420,000 associated with that of Sinclair. The ramifications of the worldwide Scottish clan and family associations are far reaching and extraordinary. No other nation has such a groundswell of organised family linkage or such an international heritage.

In April 2005 Rosslyn Chapel was voted an icon of Scotland by the judging panel of *Scotland Magazine*, which, in addition to its UK circulation, is distributed extensively across North America. Andrew Russell, Chairman of the Rosslyn Chapel Project Group, accompanied by Helen, Countess of Rosslyn, attended a glitzy awards ceremony held at the Waldorf Astoria in New York. This Heart of Scotland Icon Award is presented as part of America's annual Tartan Week celebrations and, in this case, recognised Rosslyn Chapel as 'a tourist attraction or place in Scotland which best captures the true nature of Scotland'.

Admittedly the vote was to a degree prompted by the success of *The Da Vinci Code* – which had sold 25 million copies in forty-four languages over two years – and the subsequent upsurge of international interest in the chapel, but it is also fair to say that the judges were unanimous in their affection for a building which they had all, with one exception, visited at some stage in their lives.

Moreover, the publicity surrounding the chapel could not have come at a more beneficial time for the Rosslyn Chapel Trust since over the past eight years the entire building has required substantial and costly renovation. To a great extent this has been funded by the National Heritage Lottery Fund, the Eastern Scotland European Partnership and Historic Scotland, but the ongoing costs of maintaining such a fragile survivor of the fifteenth century are enormous.

On a conservative estimate, over £3 million requires to be raised to fund the repair work which began in 1997, starting with a purpose-designed steel structure being erected by the engineer John Addison to enable the stone roof to dry out thoroughly. Since then an overlay of Caithness slate has been placed over the existing crypt roof, and the priest's cell, with two more modern buildings beside the crypt being made functional. Although concern has been voiced at the startling increase in visitor numbers since the publication of *The Da Vinci Code* and the numerous Templar-related books, nobody is going to say that the response has been entirely unwelcome. The accumulative entry fees have been the chapel's salvation.

Baron St Clair Bonde has been involved as a trustee of the Rosslyn Chapel Trust since its formation in 1995, and finds the chapel the most enchanting place regardless of what might or might not be hidden away beneath it. He has a feeling, however, that at some time in the future all will be revealed, but that, he insists, need not necessarily be a bad thing: 'If that revelation can help join the gap between the three monotheistic religions that all believe in the same God, albeit from different angles, that would be quite something!' In the meantime, Rosslyn Chapel remains a working church, with Sunday services, a priest, and a congregation, many of whom understandably resent the intrusion of the occasional tourist with a camera or metal detector during their weekly devotions.

In a published series of five sermons, the Revd Michael Fass, the priest in charge, thoughtfully explains his response to a situation which has only recently arisen over the years of his tenure. He has learned that when people say, 'This place is not really a church, it's just disguised as one!' or 'I know the Head of God is here – where can I find it?', it is best to challenge them about their understanding of God.[2]

'What is the role and mission of the remnant church in this place and how should we respond to such pressures?' he also asks. Michael Fass remains passionate that Rosslyn Chapel should fulfil its historic role and 'not be a place of unhealed or false memories, nor of secrets and sensational speculation of "esoteric" enquiry –

for there are no secrets here – and not of the New Age search for personal satisfaction, but rather that it should be a place of Healing, Reconciliation and Prayer.'

As for those evasive treasures which the sleeping St Clair knights of Rosslyn guard deep within their chapel vaults, will some future generation with superior technology one day unearth the Ark of the Covenant or Holy Grail, in whatever form it takes? Or the Holy Rude of Scotland, brought to Rosslyn for safekeeping in the sixteenth century? Now that might be a more realistic prize. Perhaps even the head-shrine of St Margaret, given Father Richard Hay's close connection with the Scots colleges in both Douai and Paris?[3] Fabulous as they are, however, these are only physical curiosities belonging to bygone ages. Taken in their totality, Rosslyn Chapel, Rosslyn Castle and the glen of the River North Esk are the real treasures here.

Ultimately, Michael Fass is right. What really matters is the maintenance and development of this place in its historic and modern role as the location of the divine, and of the holy spirit in the story of Jesus, for which purpose it was built. 'So we should not focus unduly upon the current restoration and touristic or financial aims, which are of course a laudable means to an end, but not the end in itself,' he says.

No one can accurately predict the future of Rosslyn Chapel, its owners, its congregation, its castle or the landscape which surrounds it. All the same, it would be gratifying to think that its beauty, and the fascination that this engenders, will continue unspoiled for at least another five hundred years and survive, as surely it will, the cacophony of indulgent and often absurd speculation which has engulfed it at the beginning of the third millennium.

Notes to the text

Complete citations can be found within the bibliography.

CHAPTER ONE

1 Madge Old, *A Short History to Celebrate the Centenary of Rosslyn Church.*
2 Father Richard Augustine Hay, *Genealogie of the Sainteclaires of Rosslyn.*
3 Will Grant, *Rosslyn: Its Castle, Chapel and Scenic Lore.*
4 Revd John Thompson, *The 1893 Guide to Rosslyn Chapel, Castle and Hawthornden.*
5 *Ibid.*
6 *Ibid.*
7 George F Black PhD, *The Surnames of Scotland: Their Origin, Meaning and History.*
8 Revd John Thompson, *The 1893 Guide to Rosslyn Chapel, Castle and Hawthornden.*

CHAPTER TWO

1 Glyn S Burgess (trans.), *The History of the Norman People: Wace's Roman de Rou.* Part II.
2 Gabriel Ronay, *The Lost King of England: The East European Adventures of Edward the Exile.*
3 Father Richard Augustine Hay, *Genealogie of the Sainteclaires of Rosslyn.*

4 Niven Sinclair, notes provided.
5 David McRoberts, *St Margaret of Scotland.*

CHAPTER THREE

1 Terry Jones and Alan Ereira, *Crusades.*
2 *Ibid.*
3 Lionel Smithett Lewis, *St Joseph of Arimathea at Glastonbury.*
4 Samuel W Mitcham Jnr, *Hitler's Field Marshals: The men ordered to conquer the world.*
5 John Calvin, *Traites des Reliques.*
6 Terry Jones and Alan Ereira, *Crusades.*

CHAPTER FOUR

1 Father Richard Augustine Hay, *Account of the Templars together with an Account of the Joannites or Knights of St John.*
2 Helen Nicholson, *The Knights Templar: A New History.*
3 Evelyn Lord, *The Knights Templar in Britain.*
4 John Martine, *Reminiscences and Notices of the Parishes of the Counties of Haddington.*
5 Evelyn Lord, *The Knights Templar in Britain.*
6 M Barber, *The Trial of the Templars.*
7 Helen Nicholson, *The Knights Templar: A New History.*
8 Evelyn Lord, *The Knights Templar in Britain.*

CHAPTER FIVE

1 From the list of names published by the Bannatyne Club of Edinburgh in 1834.
2 John Ritchie, 'Battle of Roslin 1303', (www.sinclair.quarterman.org/ history and www.thesonsofscotland.co.uk), and 'The Battle of Roslin', Gems of Midlothian (local marketing initiative).
3 Isabel Carton-Downs and Egan-Oldfield, *The Carlton: Marlatts Descendants of De Marle.*
4 Edinburgh City Libraries, *The Battle of Roslin fought on the Plains of Roslin 1303.*
5 Lloyd Laing, *The Picts and the Scots.*

[6] CH Lawrence, *Mediaeval Monasticism.*

[7] Father Richard Augustine Hay, *Genealogie of the Sainteclaires of Rosslyn.*

[8] JG Lockhart, *Curses, Lucks and Talismans.*

CHAPTER SIX

[1] Father Richard Augustine Hay, *Genealogie of the Sainteclaires of Rosslyn.* He says that he was Sir William's prisoner, not Sir Henry's, but the dates do not ring true.

[2] Andrew Sinclair, *The Sword and the Grail.*

[3] Father Richard Augustine Hay, *Genealogie of the Sainteclaires of Rosslyn.*

[4] *Ibid.*

[5] Revd John Thompson, *The 1893 Guide to Rosslyn Chapel, Castle and Hawthornden.*

CHAPTER SEVEN

[1] Helge and Anne Ingstad, *The Norse Discovery of America.*

[2] The author-explorer Tim Severin sailed a leather boat across the Atlantic Ocean in the wake of St Brendan the Navigator.

[3] Wallace Clark, 'The Lord of the Isles Voyage'.

[4] Andrew Sinclair, *The Sword and the Grail.*

[5] 'Dello Scoprimento dell isole Frislanda, Eslanda, Engroulanda, Estotilanda e icario fatto sotto ile Polo artico da due fratelli Zeni. M. Nicolo il K. e M. Antonio.' (Venice 1558). In 1998, the Zeno Map was republished along with a booklet entitled Sinclair's Exploration of America by the Prince Henry Project Committee in Massachusetts, USA, to celebrate the six-hundredth anniversary of his voyage.

[6] The Money Pit on Oak Island has fascinated generations of treasure hunters from American President Franklin D Roosevelt to the Hollywood actor Errol Flynn. Treasure hunters while excavating during the mid 1860s encountered soggy ground. This was not too surprising because the pit was only 500 feet from the coastline and high tide of the ocean was about at the 32 foot level. At 98 feet they struck an extra-hard surface. They took the rest of the day off and the next

morning found that the shaft of the pit was filled with sea water to the 32-foot level. They had inadvertently opened a series of channels to the beach that had been installed as a booby trap. This is yet another possible resting place for the lost wealth of the Knights Templar.

7 Father Richard Augustine Hay, *Genealogie of the Sainteclaires of Rosslyn*.

CHAPTER EIGHT

1 TS Muir, 'Descriptive Notices of some Ancient Parochial and Collegiate Churches of Scotland' in *Gazeteer of Scotland*, 1885.

2 *Ibid.*

3 David Hume of Godscroft (*c*.1560–1630) was secretary to the 8th Earl of Angus. He wrote histories of the House of Douglas and of the House of Wedderburn.

4 Father Richard Augustine Hay, *Genealogie of the Sainteclaires of Rosslyn*.

5 Revd Michael Fass, *Faith and Place: Six centuries of Christian Witness*.

6 AJ Stewart, *Falcon*.

7 AJ Stewart, *Died 1513; Born 1929*.

8 Hugh Pesketh, Family tree of the St Clairs, privately commissioned by Baron Bonde and family.

9 Agnes Mure Mackenzie, *The Kingdom of Scotland*.

CHAPTER NINE

1 Since the Holy Rude had been brought back to Scotland for the first time by his ancestor, Sir Henry St Clair, it seems likely, given the emotional attachment involved, that Prince William would have requested it when he too attended the English Court as Scottish Ambassador.

2 Incensed at the Scots' refusal to betroth the infant Queen Mary to Prince Edward of England, his father, Henry VIII of England, in 1544 ordered the Earl of Hertford to invade Scotland and to 'Sack Leith and burn and subvert it and all the rest, putting man, woman

and child to fire and sword without exception.' The entire Old Town and Edinburgh Castle was destroyed, excepting St Margaret's Chapel, which still stands today. This period became known as the 'Rough Wooing'.

3 The Battle of Pinkie, fought along the banks of the River Esk near Musselburgh on 10 September 1547, was the last battle to be fought between the Scottish and the English Royal armies and the first 'modern' battle to be fought in the British Isles. It was a catastrophic defeat for the Scots, caused by poor discipline and weak command. In Scotland it is known as Black Saturday.

4 Father Richard Augustine Hay, *Genealogie of the Sainteclaires of Rosslyn.*

5 Philip Coppens, *The Stone Puzzle of Rosslyn Chapel.*

CHAPTER TEN

1 John Robertson and Edward Black, *Scotsman,* 11 Dec 2002.

2 James Maidment (*c.*1795–1879) was a lawyer and scholar who dedicated his life to antiquarian research. He was the principal editor of *Kay's Portraits* (A&C Black, 1837).

3 Father Richard Augustine Hay, *Genealogie of the Sainteclaires of Rosslyn.*

4 George S Draffen, *Pour la Foy.*

5 5th Earl of Rosslyn, *My Gamble with Life.*

CHAPTER ELEVEN

1 Professor Geoffrey Barrow has been president of the Scottish History Society, the Scottish Record Society, and the Saltire Society (now Hon. President). He was Joint Literary Director, Royal Historical Society, 1964–74; Vice-President, 1980–85. He jointly edited the *Scottish Historical Review,* 1974–79. He was a member of the Royal Commission on Historical Manuscripts, 1983–90.

2 John, Master of St Clair, Autobiography, 1715. This extract is quoted in the editor's notes for the 1805 edition of *Scott's Poetical Works.*

CHAPTER TWELVE

[1] Albert Krantz, *Saxonia.*

[2] Gypsies have usually adopted the religion of their country of residence; probably the greater number are Roman Catholic or Orthodox Eastern Christian. Every May they gather in the south of France from all over the world for a pilgrimage to Saintes-Maries-de-la-Mer. Nowadays they make their living as metalworkers, singers, dancers, musicians, horse dealers, and auto mechanics.

[3] The Golden Calf was a deity borrowed from the Egyptians to become an object of worship among Hebrews.

CHAPTER THIRTEEN

[1] Presbytery Notes of Dalkeith 1580–1600.

[2] Revd John Thompson, *The 1893 Guide to Rosslyn Chapel, Castle and Hawthornden.*

[3] Revd Prof. HJ Lawlor, DD, FSA Scot, 'Notes on the Library of the Sinclairs of Rosslyn' in *Proceedings of the Society of Antiquaries in Scotland* 1879–98.

CHAPTER FOURTEEN

[1] Sir Iain Moncreiffe of that Ilk, *Royal Highness*. See also *Blood Royal* (Sir Iain Moncreiffe and Don Pottinger).

[2] Sir Iain Moncreiffe of that Ilk, Introduction to *Debrett's Family Historian.*

[3] Arthur Herman, *How the Scots invented the Modern World.*

[4] The Gospel of Mary Magdalene was found in the Akhmim Codex, a Gnostic text of the New Testament apocrypha acquired by Dr Rheinhardt in Cairo in 1896. It was not published until 1955. http://en.wikipedia.org/wiki/1955

CHAPTER FIFTEEN

[1] In his essay on St Margaret, Queen of Scotland, reprinted by St Margaret's Dunfermline in 1993 to celebrate the saint's ninth

centenary, the historian David MacRoberts tells us that a Father James Carruthers claims to have seen the head-shrine at Douai, when he left France in 1785, which makes it being at Rosslyn unlikely. The essay can be seen online at www.ewtn.com/library/MARY/ STMARG.HTM. Father Hay's description, however, in which he suggests that some of the gemstones might have been fake, hints that it might have been copied.

CHAPTER SIXTEEN

[1] Prior to his mysterious death at the age of thirty-five, Otto Rahn (1904–38) wrote two books about the Cathars of southern France: *Kreuzzug gegen den Gral* (*Crusade Against the Grail*), and *Luzifers Hofgesinf* (*Lucifer's Court*).

[2] Jean Cocteau (1889–1963) experimented audaciously in almost every artistic medium, becoming a leader of the French avant-garde in the 1920s. His first great success was the novel *Les Enfants Terribles* (1929), which he made into a film in 1950. His films included *The Blood of a Poet* (1933), *Beauty and the Beast* (1946), and *Orphée* (1949). Among his other works are ballets, sketches, monologues, and the text (written with Stravinsky) for the opera-oratorio *Oedipus Rex* (1927).

CHAPTER SEVENTEEN

[1] Horace Bleakley, *The Story of the Beautiful Duchess.*

[2] Rosebank House has since been demolished. It was the birthplace in 1746 of the poet Hector MacNeill, editor of *Scots Magazine*, and author of such songs as 'I loved ne'er a Lassie but Ane', 'Mary of Castlecary' and 'The Plaid among the Heather'.

CHAPTER EIGHTEEN

[1] Revd Michael Fass, *Faith and Place.*

[2] VG Childe and John Taylor, *Proceedings of the Society of Antiquaries in Scotland,* 1938–39, National Library of Scotland.

CHAPTER NINETEEN

[1] 5th Earl of Rosslyn, *My Gamble with Life.*
[2] Douglas Sutherland, *The Yellow Earl.*
[3] 7th Earl of Rosslyn, *Rosslyn Chapel.*

CHAPTER TWENTY

[1] Revd John Thompson F.S.A., Chaplain to the Right Hon. Earl of Rosslyn, *The 1893 Guide to Rosslyn Chapel, Castle and Hawthornden.*
[2] Angelo Maggi, 'Poetic Stones: Roslin Chapel in Gandy's Sketchbook and Daguerre's Diorama' and 'Rosslyn Chapel: a pocket cathedral in an Earthly Paradise'.

CHAPTER TWENTY-ONE

[1] Dorothy Wordsworth (1771–1855) was the younger sister of the poet William Wordsworth. For nearly a century she was relegated to being a footnote in her brother's life. Then, in 1931, Dove Cottage, the Lake District home where Dorothy and William lived for several years, was bought by Beatrix Potter, author of *Peter Rabbit* and other children's books. In the barn, Potter found a bundle of old papers and realized that they were Dorothy's journals. Her discovery was published in 1933 as *The Grasmere Journal.* The journal eloquently described her day-to-day life in the Lake District, long walks she and her brother took through the countryside, and detailed portraits of literary lights of the eighteenth century, including Samuel Taylor Coleridge, Sir Walter Scott and Charles Lamb.
[2] Research into the names of Celtic gods and goddesses shows that one Celtic deity, Viridios, has a common meaning, 'Green Man', in both Celtic and Latin, the two languages being related.
[3] Artichokes were a popular motif symbolising protection, strength and courage.

CHAPTER TWENTY-TWO

[1] 5th Earl of Rosslyn, *My Gamble with Life.*

CHAPTER TWENTY-THREE

[1] Midlothian Strategic Surveys, Draft Report: Roslin Conservation Area.

[2] Revd Michael Fass, *Faith and Place.*

[3] Father Richard Hay returned to Scotland around 1719 and died in poverty approximately seventeen years later living in Edinburgh's Cowgate. His complete writings are to be found in the National Library of Scotland. Otherwise, see the edited *Genealogie of the Sainteclaires of Rosslyn* published by the Grand Lodge of Scotland 2002.

Bibliography

Albany, Prince Michael of, *The Forgotten Monarchy of Scotland* (Chrysalis/Vega Books, 2002)

Baigent, Michael; Lincoln, Henry & Leigh, Richard *The Temple and the Lodge* (Jonathan Cape, 1989)

Baigent, Michael; Lincoln, Henry & Leigh, Richard *The Holy Blood and The Holy Grail* (Jonathan Cape, 1982; Arrow Books Ltd, 1996)

Barber, M, *The Trial of the Templars* (CUP, 1993)

Black, George F, *The Surnames of Scotland: Their Origin, Meaning and History* (New York Public Library, 1946; Birlinn, 1993)

Bleakley, Horace, *The Story of the Beautiful Duchess* (Constable, 1907)

Brown, Dan, *The Da Vinci Code* (Corgi Adult, 2003)

Burgess, Glyn S (trans.), *The History of the Norman People – Wace's Roman de Rou* (The Boydell Press, 2004)

Calvin, John, *Traites des Reliques* (Geneva, 1617)

Carton-Downs, Isabel and Egan-Oldfield, *The Carlton: Marlatts Descendants of De Marle* (self-published, 1980)

Clark, Wallace, 'Lord of the Isles Voyage', *Leinster Leader*, 1992

Coppens, Philip, *The Stone Puzzle of Rosslyn Chapel* (Frontier Publishing and Adventures Unlimited Press, 2004)

Cox, Simon, *Cracking the Da Vinci Code* (Michael O'Mara Books, 2004)

Draffen, George S, *Pour la Foy. A short history of the Great Priory of Scotland* (David Winter & Son, 1949)

Dunnett, Dorothy, *Gemini* (Michael Joseph, 1999)

Fass, Revd Michael, *Faith and Place: Six Centuries of Christian Witness*, (Congregation of St Michael's, Rosslyn Chapel, 2003)

Gardner, Laurence, *The Bloodline of the Holy Grail* (Element Books, 2002)

——, *Lost Secrets of the Sacred Ark* (Element Books, 2003)

——, *The Magdalene Legacy: The Jesus and Mary Bloodline Conspiracy* (Harper Collins, 2005)

Grant, Will, *Rosslyn: Its Castle, Chapel and Scenic Lore* (Dysart & Rosslyn Estates/ MacNiven and Wallace, 1947)

Guirdham, Arthur, *The Cathars and Reincarnation: The record of a past life in 13th century France* (Neville Spearman, 1970)

Hay, Father Richard Augustine, *Genealogie of the Sainteclaires of Rosslyn*, ed. Brother Robert LD Cooper, trans. from the Latin Brother John Wade, (The Grand Lodge of Scotland, 1835, 2002)

——, *Account of the Templars together with an Account of the Joannites or Knights of St John*, ed. James Maidment (Edinburgh, 1823)

Herman, Arthur, *How the Scots invented the Modern World* (Crown Publications, 2001)

Ingstad, Helge and Anne, *The Norse Discovery of America: The Historical Background and the Evidence of the Norse Settlement Discovered in Newfoundland* (Universitetsforlaget, Oslo, 1986)

Jones, Terry, and Ereira, Alan, *Crusades* (BBC Books, 1994)

Knight, Christoper & Robert Lomas, *The Hiram Key: Pharaohs, Freemasons and the Discovery of the Secret Scrolls of Christ* (Century, 1996)

Krantz, Albert, *Saxonia* (Cologne, 1520)

Laidler, Keith, *The Head of God – The Lost Treasures of the Templars* (Orion, 1999)

Laing, Lloyd, *The Picts and the Scots* (Sutton Publishing, 2001)

Lawrence, CH, *Mediaeval Monasticism* (Longman, 1984)

Lewis, Lionel Smithett, *St Joseph of Arimathea at Glastonbury* (Lutterworth Press, 2004)

Lincoln, Henry, *Key to the Sacred Pattern: the Untold Story of Rennes-le-Château* (Windrush Press, 1997)

Lockhart, JG, *Curses, Lucks and Talismans* (Geoffrey Bles, 1938)

Lord, Evelyn, *The Knights Templar in Britain* (Pearson Longman, 2002)

McRoberts, David, *St Margaret of Scotland* (St Margaret's, 1993)

Maggi, Angelo, 'Poetic Stones: Roslin Chapel in Gandy's Sketchbook and Daguerre's Diorama' in *Journal of the Society of Architectural Historians* (Sept. 1999)

——, 'Rosslyn Chapel: a pocket cathedral in an Earthly Paradise' in *Rosslyn: Country of Painter and Poet* (National Gallery of Scotland, 2002)

Mann, William F, *The Knights Templar in the New World* (Inner Traditions International, 2004)

Markale, Jean, *Montsegur and the Mystery of the Cathars* (Inner Traditions International, 2003)

—, *The Church of Mary Magdalene: The Sacred Feminine and the Treasures of Rennes-Le-Château* (Inner Traditions International, 2004)

Martine, John, *Reminiscences and Notices of the Parishes and Counties of Haddington* (East Lothian Council Literary Service, 1999)

Midlothian Strategic Surveys, 'Draft Report: Roslin Conservation Area'

Mitcham Jnr, Samuel W, *Hitler's Field Marshals: The men ordered to conquer the world* (Grafton Books, 1989)

Moncreiffe of that Ilk, Sir Iain, Introduction to *Debrett's Family Historian* (Debrett's 1981)

——, *Royal Highness – Ancestry of the Royal Child* (Hamish Hamilton, 1982)

—— & Don Pottinger, *Blood Royal* (Thomas Nelson & Sons, 1956)

Munro, Graeme, *Esk Valley Study Day Lecture* (Historic Scotland, 1998)

Mure Mackenzie, Agnes, *The Kingdom of Scotland* (Chambers, 1947)

Nicholson, Helen, *The Knights Templar: A New History* (Sutton Publishing, 2001)

Old, Madge, *A Short History to Celebrate the Centenary of Rosslyn Church* (Roslin Public Library, 1981)

Rahn, Otto, *Kreuzzug gegen den Gral* (*Against the Grail*) (1933; republished Pardes, 1964)

——, *Luzifers Hofgesinf* (*Lucifer's Court*) (Berlin, 1937)

Rankin, Ian, *The Falls* (Orion, 2001)

Robertson, Ian & Oxbrow, Mark, *Rosslyn and The Grail* (Mainstream, 2005)

Ronay, Gabriel, *The Lost King of England: The East European Adventures of Edward the Exile* (Boydell Press, 2002)

Rosslyn, 5th Earl of, *My Gamble with Life* (JH Sears & Co., 1928)

Rosslyn, 7th Earl of, *Rosslyn Chapel* (Rosslyn Chapel Trust, 1996)

Rosslyn, Helen, Countess of; Maggi, Angelo & Simpson, James, *Rosslyn: Country of Painter and Poet* (National Galleries of Scotland, 1999)

Severin, Tim, *The Brendan Voyage* (Arrow Books, 1976)

Sinclair, Andrew, *The Sword and the Grail: The Story of the Grail, the Templars and the True Discovery of America* (Century, 1992)

——, *Rosslyn: The Story of Rosslyn Chapel and the True Story behind* The Da Vinci Code (Birlinn, 2005)

Smith, G Gregory, MA Edin, BA Oxon, *The Days of James iiii 1488– 1513* (David Mutt, 1900)

Sora, Steven, *The Lost Colony on the Templars* (Destiny Books, 2004)

Stewart, AJ, *Falcon: The Autobiography of His Grace James IV, King of Scots* (Peter Davies, 1970)

——, *Died 1513; Born 1929* (Macmillan, 1978)

Sutherland, Douglas, *The Yellow Earl* (Molendinar Press, 1965)

Thompson F.S.A., Revd John, *The 1893 Guide to Rosslyn Chapel, Castle and Hawthornden* (Country Books, 2004)

Wallace-Murphy, Tim, *The Templar Legacy and the Masonic Inheritance Within Rosslyn Chapel* (Friends of Rosslyn, 1994)

—— & Hopkins, Marilyn, *Rosslyn: Guardian of the Secrets of the Holy Grail* (Element Books, 1999)

Index